THE ULTIMATE NEW YORK CITY TRIVIA

THE ULTIMATE NEW YORK CITY TRIVIA

COMPILED BY HY BRETT

Rutledge Hill Press
Nashville, Tennessee

Copyright © 1997 by Hy Brett.
All rights reserved. Written permission must be secured from the publisher to use or reproduce any part of this book, except for brief quotations in critical reviews and articles.

Published in Nashville, Tennessee, by Rutledge Hill Press,
211 Seventh Avenue North, Nashville, Tennessee 37219.
Distributed in Canada by H. B. Fenn & Company, Ltd.,
34 Nixon Road, Bolton, Ontario L7E 1W2.

Typography by D&T/Bailey Typesetting, Inc., Nashville, Tennessee.

Excerpts from *Where to Go: A Guide to Manhattan's Toilets* by Vicki Rovere, © 1991 by Vicki Rovere, used by permission.

Eau de New York written by the editor.

Library of Congress Cataloging-in-Publication Data

Brett, Hy.
    The ultimate New York City trivia book / compiled by Hy Brett.
      p. cm.
      ISBN 1-55853-499-7 (pbk.)
    1. New York (N.Y.)—Miscellanea. I. Title.
F128.3.B79   1997
974.7'1—dc21   97-26873
                                                                         CIP

Printed in the United States of America.
1 2 3 4 5 6 7 8 9 — 01 00 99 98 97

PREFACE

Thanks to the movies and television, and also to photographs in newspapers, magazines, and books, probably everyone knows what New York City looks like. With its Statue of Liberty and skyscrapers, vast parks, grand avenues, museums and theaters, it is like no other city in the world. New York City has been five hundred years in the making, and its population of more than 7.5 million represents every race, religion, and nationality in the world.

Created by a New Yorker, this book informs readers near and far about the people and events that make New York City unique and exciting. No one feels like a stranger for long in New York City because of the variety of its offerings, and I hope that, wherever they are, readers will soon feel that they are New Yorkers of a sort.

To my wife, Barbara, in Brooklyn, New York,
and, now far from New York City, but always a part of it,
to my children Jennifer and David, and my grandchildren
Hilary and Samuel in Nashville,
and to my children Steven and Lynn in Skokie, Illinois

TABLE OF CONTENTS

PREFACE	5
GEOGRAPHY	9
WHERE TO GO IN NEW YORK	37
ENTERTAINMENT	41
HISTORY	75
ARTS & LITERATURE	117
SPORTS & LEISURE	159
SCIENCE & NATURE	193

God made the country, but man made the town.
—*William Cowper*

GEOGRAPHY

CHAPTER ONE

East Side, West Side,
All around the town.

—Blake & Lawlor

Q. What is the official name of New York City?

A. The City of Greater New York.

Q. The latitude and the longitude of New York City are what?

A. 40° 47′ by 73° 58′.

Q. Where is the city's official site on the Internet?

A. http://www.ci.nyc.ny.us.

Q. What is the city's population?

A. According to the 1990 U.S. census, 7.3 million and at least 250,000 illegal immigrants.

Q. How many buildings are there in the city?

A. Almost one million.

Geography

Q. How many miles of streets are there in New York?
A. 6,400.

Q. What are the five boroughs of New York City?
A. The Bronx, Brooklyn, Manhattan, Queens, and Staten Island.

Q. Below ground are how many miles of telephone wire?
A. About 20 million.

Q. Which is the only borough connected to the mainland?
A. The Bronx.

Q. How many islands are part of the city?
A. Fifty.

Q. How many bridges are there in the city?
A. Two thousand.

Q. Where is the highest natural spot in Manhattan?
A. Fort Tryon Park at 268 feet.

Geography

Q. How long and wide is Manhattan?

A. Twelve miles long and two miles wide.

Q. What is the longest street in New York City and also in the world?

A. Broadway stretches 150 miles between Bowling Green in Manhattan to Albany, New York.

Q. Where is the shortest street in the city?

A. Edgar Street in Lower Manhattan. It is just a few feet between Trinity Place and Greenwich Street.

Q. When was the name of Longacre Square in Midtown Manhattan changed to Times Square?

A. April 8, 1904.

Q. Boulevards commemorate what three noted African Americans in Manhattan?

A. Duke Ellington, Dr. Martin Luther King Jr., and the Reverend Adam Clayton Powell Jr.

Q. On what street, in 1657, was the first stone pavement laid?

A. Stone Street in Lower Manhattan.

Q. What is Broadway's nickname?

A. The Great White Way.

Wall Street in 1924, looking west toward Broadway from the U.S. Treasury Building (Today it is called Federal Hall National Memorial.). In the distance is historic Trinity Church, constructed in 1846.

GEOGRAPHY

Q. For what was Wall Street named?

A. The 2,340-foot fortification, built in 1653, that protected the Dutch from English and Native-American invaders.

Q. Why is New York City called the Big Apple?

A. Jazz musicians considered it the biggest and juiciest gig on the tree of success.

Q. Before the Big Apple caught on, what were other nicknames for the city?

A. Gotham, Empire City, The City Beautiful, or The Big Town.

Q. Who created the Big Apple advertising campaign in 1971?

A. Charles Gillett, president of the New York Convention and Visitors Bureau.

Q. How many miles of subway track are there in the city?

A. 722.

Q. Why are there always flags hanging outside the Waldorf-Astoria Hotel?

A. To indicate the presence of foreign VIPs.

Q. What is the name of the only high-rise apartment building in Chinatown?

A. Confucius Plaza

GEOGRAPHY

Q. Early in the twentieth century, where was Newspaper Row, the site of the influential publications owned by such entrepreneurs as William Randolph Hearst and Joseph Pulitzer?

A. Park Row near city hall.

Q. What city planner created Manhattan's pattern of north-south avenues and east-west streets?

A. John Randall Jr. in 1807.

Q. How does traffic flow on numbered streets in Manhattan, most of which are one way?

A. Odd-numbered streets run west; even-numbered streets run east.

Q. Subway trains stop at how many stations?

A. 469.

Q. A green globe outside a subway entrance means what?

A. It is staffed twenty-four hours a day.

Q. What does a red globe outside a subway entrance mean?

A. The entrance is closed or unavailable.

Q. The present subway system is a combination of what three separate entities?

A. IRT (Interborough Rapid Transit), BMT (Brooklyn-Manhattan Transit), and the Independent Subway System.

GEOGRAPHY

Q. Once you have bought a subway token, how far can you ride?

A. Back and forth for as long as you like.

Q. Atop what building in Brooklyn is the world's largest clock?

A. The Williamsburgh Savings Bank. Each of the clock's four sides has a diameter of twenty-seven feet.

Q. Since its completion in 1973, what structure has superseded the Empire State Building as the tallest in town?

A. The World Trade Center in Lower Manhattan has 110 stories reaching a height of 1,377 feet.

Q. How tall is the Empire State Building?

A. 102 stories and 1,250 feet.

Q. What are the Lower Manhattan areas south of Houston Street and north of Houston Street known as?

A. Soho and Noho.

Q. Where is Tribeca in Lower Manhattan?

A. In a triangle below Canal Street on the West Side.

Q. What north-south thoroughfares separate the East and West sides in Manhattan?

A. Broadway in Lower Manhattan. Fifth Avenue in Upper Manhattan.

Geography

Q. For what very different attributes are the Lower East Side and the Upper East Side best known?

A. Great poverty and great wealth respectively.

Q. Because of notorious activities that went on there, what thoroughfare gentrified its name to Marketfield Street in the late 1700s?

A. Petticoat Lane.

Q. What and where is Alphabet City?

A. Avenues A through D on the Lower East Side.

Q. What are the four bodies of water that surround Manhattan?

A. The Hudson, Harlem, and East Rivers, and New York Bay.

Q. How long is the Hudson River?

A. It runs 315 miles from Mount Marcy in the Adirondacks to New York Bay.

Q. What is the year's biggest event in Rockefeller Center?

A. Installation and lighting of the Christmas tree in the plaza.

Q. Where is Millionaires' Row?

A. Fifth Avenue from Sixtieth Street to about Eighty-fifth Street.

Geography

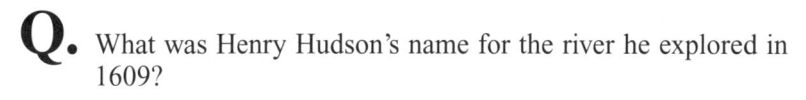

Q. What was Henry Hudson's name for the river he explored in 1609?

A. Great River of the Mountains.

Q. Though you cannot get one when it is raining or you are in a hurry, how many licensed taxis are there?

A. Almost twelve thousand.

Q. What are unlicensed taxis called?

A. Gypsies.

Q. New York's taxi drivers speak how many languages?

A. Sixty.

Q. Tourists develop stiff necks because they are tempted to stare up at how many skyscrapers?

A. About two hundred.

Q. How many of the city's residents are Native Americans?

A. About thirty thousand.

Q. We think first of Manhattan when we think of New York City, but it contains only what percent of the city's population?

A. 20 percent.

— 17 —

Geography

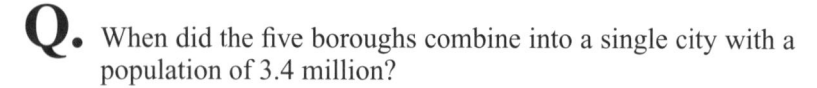

Q. When did the five boroughs combine into a single city with a population of 3.4 million?

A. January 1, 1898.

Q. Who was the city's first mayor after the boroughs were combined?

A. Robert A. van Wyck.

Q. What is the size of New York City?

A. Three hundred and four square miles.

Q. How many people visited the city in 1996?

A. About thirty million.

Q. Though you would not think so when you are trying to make a quick reservation, how many hotel rooms are there in the city?

A. About sixty thousand.

Q. What street along the Hudson River has long symbolized wealth and gracious living?

A. Riverside Drive.

Q. What do New Yorkers still call the Avenue of the Americas?

A. Sixth Avenue.

GEOGRAPHY

The Boroughs of New York City

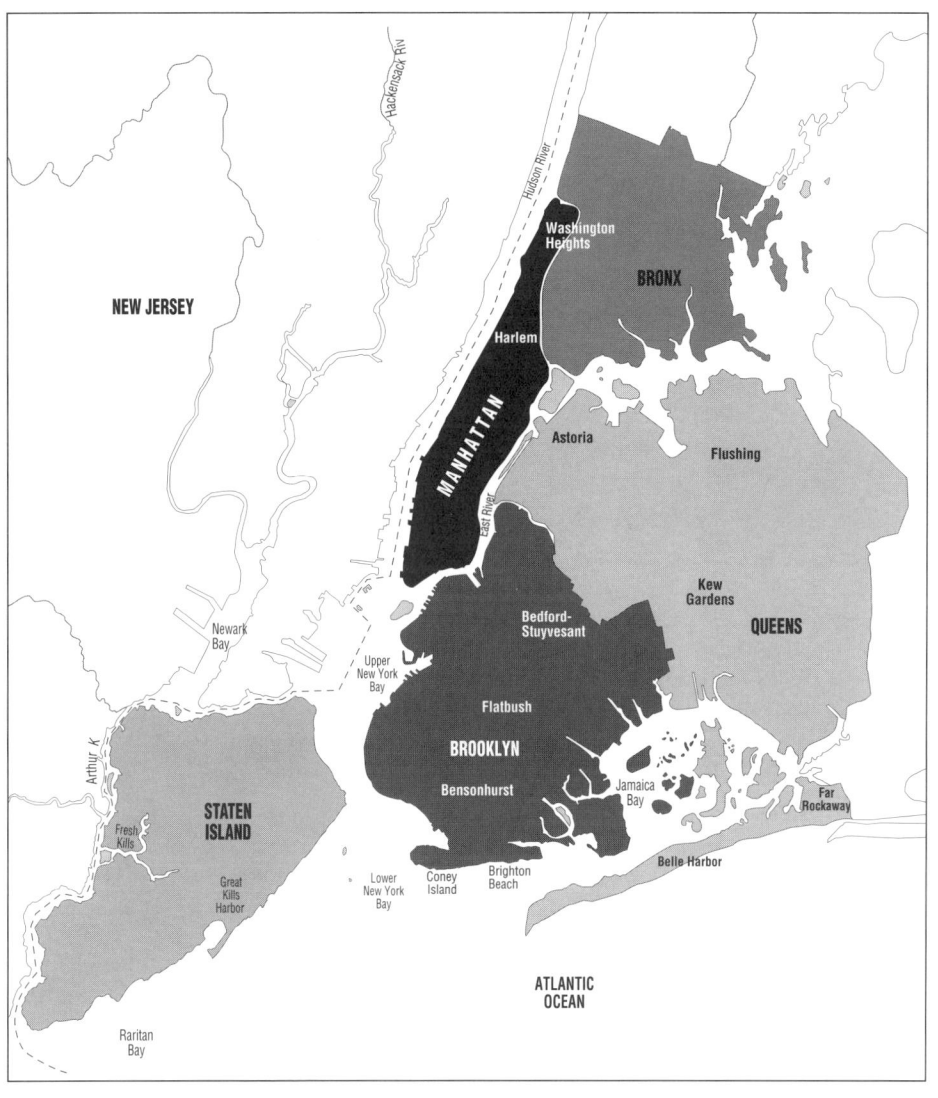

GEOGRAPHY

Q. What and where is Yorkville in Manhattan?

A. A German and Middle European area, which is between East Seventy-first and East Ninety-sixth Streets, from Lexington Avenue to the East River.

Q. Despite its recent gentrification of sorts, for what will the Bowery always be famous?

A. Vagrants and cheap lodging houses.

Q. What Manhattan building in the style of ancient Rome, designed by Stanford White in 1893, became the model for trustworthy banks all over the land?

A. The Bowery Savings Bank.

Q. Where in Manhattan is the neighborhood of Murray Hill?

A. From Twenty-seventh to Forty-second Streets, and from Third Avenue to Sixth Avenues.

Q. Where in Lower Manhattan is Greenwich Village, the traditional home of artists, writers, and actors?

A. From Broadway west to the Hudson River and from West Houston Street north to West Fourteenth Street.

Q. What Native-American village was in the area of Greenwich Village before the arrival of the Dutch and English?

A. Sappanikan.

Q. Where in Lower Manhattan is the East Village?

A. From Broadway east to the East River and from East Houston north to East Fourteenth Street.

GEOGRAPHY

Q. Where did Walt Whitman and Ralph Waldo Emerson hang out in Greenwich Village?

A. At Pfaff's Tavern.

Q. For whom is Horatio Street in Greenwich Village named?

A. Gen. Horatio Gates, a commander in the Revolutionary War.

Q. Near what Greenwich Village square was the original Circle in the Square Theater, specializing in the plays of Eugene O'Neill?

A. Sheridan Square.

Q. T. S. Eliot, a Nobel laureate and poet, lived on what alliterative street in Greenwich Village?

A. Patchin Place.

Q. What presidents have squares named for them in New York?

A. Abraham Lincoln and George Washington.

Q. The site of Washington Square Park was used for what two activities from 1789 until 1823?

A. Burying paupers and hanging criminals.

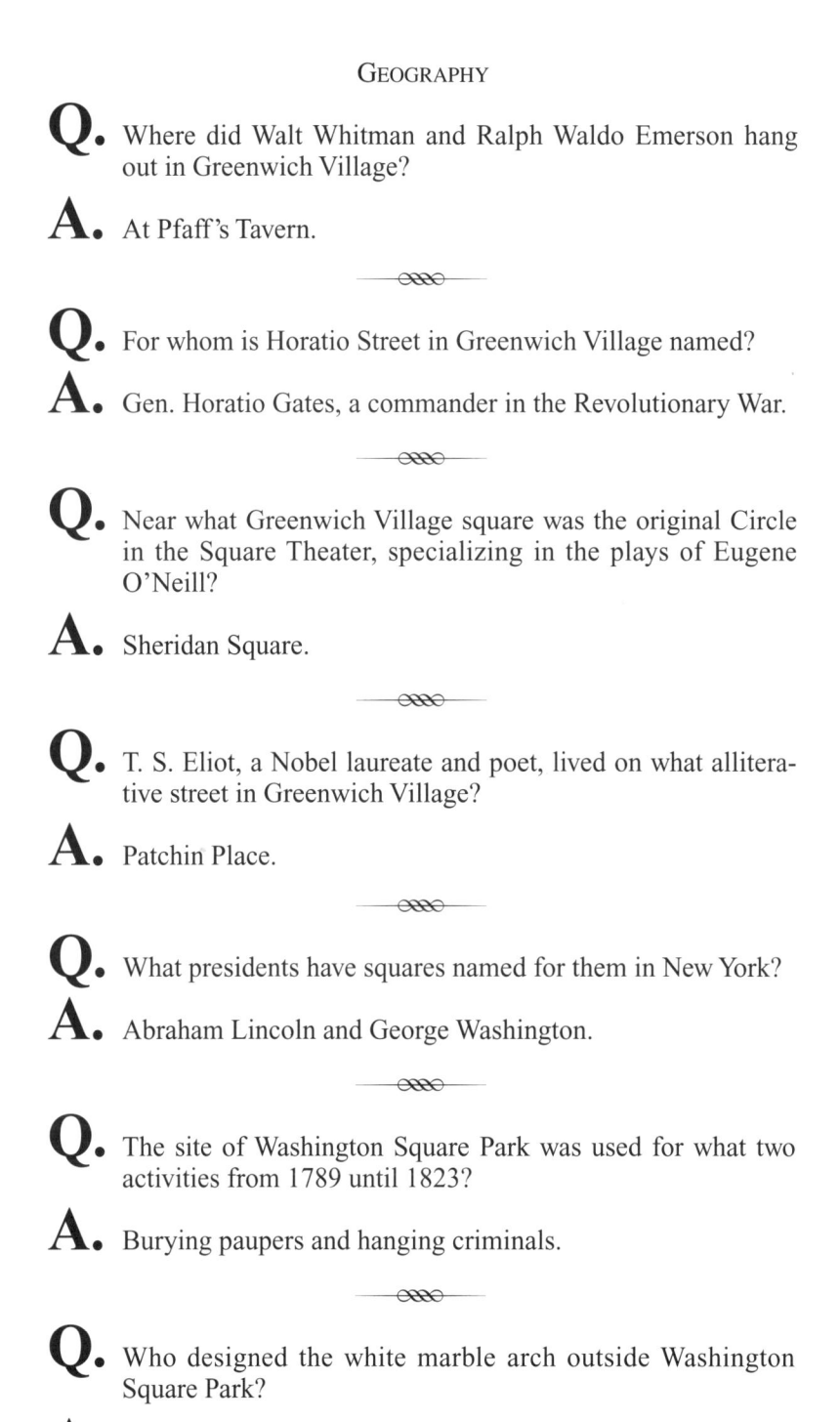

Q. Who designed the white marble arch outside Washington Square Park?

A. Stanford White.

Geography

Q. Stanford White, the city's most prolific architect, designed what landmark residential area in Harlem?

A. Strivers' Row, West 138th and 139th Streets, between Seventh and Eighth Avenues.

Q. What explorer has a circle named for him in Manhattan?

A. Christopher Columbus at the intersection of Broadway, West Fifty-ninth Street and Eighth Avenue.

Q. Now gentrified and full of tall office buildings, Third Avenue in Manhattan will always be famous for what structure of yesteryear?

A. Its elevated railroad.

Q. What was an early name of Third Avenue?

A. The Boston Post Road.

Q. Chelsea, on Manhattan's West Side from West Fourteenth through West Twenty-third Streets, is named for whom or what?

A. A London neighborhood famed for flowers and charm.

Q. Where was the red-light district, called the Tenderloin, during the nineteenth century?

A. Between Twenty-third and Forty-second Streets, from Fifth to Seventh Avenues.

Q. Where is Hell's Kitchen?

A. Manhattan in the West Thirties and Forties, from Eighth Avenue to the Hudson River.

Geography

Q. What and where is Hell's Gate?

A. A turbulent channel where the East and Harlem Rivers meet between Astoria, Queens, and Ward's Island.

Q. Where in Manhattan is Dante Park?

A. At the intersection of Broadway, Columbus Avenue, and West Sixty-fourth Street.

Q. What was Tin Pan Alley?

A. The songwriting industry centered in Times Square.

Q. Established in 1821 on South Street in Lower Manhattan, what is the largest fish distribution outlet on the East Coast?

A. The Fulton Fish Market.

Q. Seafood lovers can eat at what two historic restaurants near the fish market?

A. Sloppy Louie's and Sweets.

Q. Located on West Ninety-fifth Street and Broadway is what legendary theater devoted to film classics?

A. The Thalia.

Q. Where is Harlem?

A. In Manhattan from West 155th Street south to West 110th Street and East Ninety-sixth Street.

The main facade of Grand Central Station in 1924, facing down Park Avenue. Underwood Photo Archives, S.F.

Q. For what is Harlem named?

A. A city in Holland.

Q. What facility for travelers was built in 1871?

A. Grand Central Depot, later to become Grand Central Station.

Q. What is the longest suspension bridge in the city and country?

A. The Verrazano-Narrows, which is 4,260 feet long.

Q. Spanning New York Bay, the Verrazano-Narrows Bridge connects what boroughs?

A. Brooklyn and Staten Island.

Q. The Triborough Bridge connects what three boroughs?

A. Manhattan, the Bronx, and Queens.

GEOGRAPHY

Q. What local engineer designed the Triborough Bridge?
A. William Goldsmith.

Q. What does the George Washington Bridge over the Hudson River connect?
A. Manhattan and New Jersey.

Q. Over the Harlem River, connecting Manhattan and the Bronx, is what bridge?
A. The Washington Bridge.

Q. How many pages of listings are there in the Manhattan Yellow Pages?
A. 1,558.

Q. What three major airports serve the city?
A. Kennedy, LaGuardia, and Newark.

Q. What was the city's first airport?
A. Floyd Bennett Field in Brooklyn.

Q. The namesake of Floyd Bennett Field performed what heroic deed?
A. He flew Admiral Byrd across the North Pole in 1926.

GEOGRAPHY

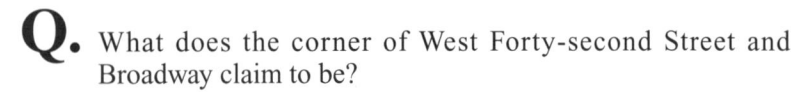

Q. What does the corner of West Forty-second Street and Broadway claim to be?

A. The crossroads of the world.

Q. Located north of Greenwich Village on Fifth and Sixth Avenues, Ladies' Mile was the site of what sort of activity in the 1800s?

A. Shopping in fancy department stores.

Q. Though Park Avenue in Midtown Manhattan is synonymous with elegance, why can it also be a place conducive to bad habits?

A. It is the headquarters of Philip Morris and Seagram's.

Q. Located in the Financial District, Maiden Lane was named for women in what occupation?

A. Washing clothes.

Q. What was the name of Exchange Place in the Financial District before the city switched from an agricultural economy?

A. Garden Street.

Q. How many of the Fortune 500 companies are headquartered in the city?

A. Sixty-five.

Q. New York is headquarters of what two organizations that fight overindulgence?

A. Alcoholics Anonymous and the National Council on Alcoholism and Drug Dependence.

— 26 —

Geography

Q. On what streets are the sides of the triangular Flatiron Building?

A. West Twenty-third Street, Broadway, and Fifth Avenue.

Q. Across the street from the Flatiron Building, who is buried in Madison Square?

A. Gen. William J. Worth, a hero of the Mexican War.

Q. Where is Turtle Bay?

A. Manhattan in the Upper East Forties, from the East River to Third Avenue.

Q. Because Turtle Bay is now filled with land, where can residents view turtles as well as sharks, seals, and hundreds of other species of marine life?

A. The New York Aquarium in Coney Island.

Q. Where and what is Coney Island?

A. In South Brooklyn. It is composed of six miles of beach, residences, and stores.

Q. How long is the Coney Island boardwalk?

A. Two miles.

Q. What is the distinction of Gravesend, once a separate village in Brooklyn?

A. Founded in 1643, it was the first colony founded by a woman, Lady Deborah Moody.

Geography

Q. For whom is the Hutchinson River in the Bronx named?

A. Anne Hutchinson, who fled to New York seeking religious freedom in 1645. She and her family were killed by Native Americans.

Q. Sutton Place, an uptown enclave for the rich near the East River, is named not for bank robber Willie Sutton but for what sharp operator in real estate?

A. Effingham Sutton.

Q. The Tavern on the Green, opened in 1934, is amid what greenery?

A. Central Park.

Q. Where in Manhattan is Central Park?

A. From West Fifty-ninth Street to Central Park North (or West 110th Street); Fifth Avenue to Central Park West (or Eighth Avenue).

Q. Seventh Avenue in Manhattan is famous as the center of what commercial enterprise?

A. The garment industry.

Q. Where in Manhattan is Washington Heights?

A. From 145th Street north to Dyckman Street and from the Harlem River west to the Hudson.

Q. Where and what is Co-Op City?

A. The East Bronx. It is the largest housing project in the city.

— 28 —

Geography

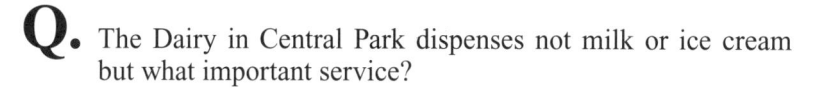

Q. The Dairy in Central Park dispenses not milk or ice cream but what important service?

A. Information about the park.

Q. Because it is named for President Franklin D. Roosevelt, a Democrat, what do Republicans persist in calling the FDR Drive?

A. The East River Drive.

Q. What is Brooklyn's nickname?

A. The Borough of Churches, because it has 725 churches.

Q. And how many churches, temples, and mosques are there in the whole city?

A. About six thousand.

Q. In what Brooklyn church is a fragment of Plymouth Rock embedded?

A. Our Lady of Lebanon on Remsen Street.

Q. Headquartered in Brooklyn Heights is what worldwide religious organization?

A. Jehovah's Witnesses.

Q. What religious movement has its world headquarters in the Crown Heights section of Brooklyn?

A. Lubavitch branch of Judaism.

Geography

Q. What is the nickname of Queens?

A. The Borough of Homes.

Q. What great sports landmark is located in Queens?

A. Shea Stadium, home of the Mets.

Q. Staten Island, also called Richmond, is how far from the rest of the city?

A. One mile from Brooklyn, five miles from Manhattan.

Q. How long and wide is Staten Island?

A. It is 13.9 miles long and 7.3 miles wide.

Q. What is the origin of the name Staten Island?

A. From the early Dutch governing body, the States General.

Q. In the late 1680s, Staten Island was a refuge for what victims of religious oppression in Europe?

A. French Huguenots.

Q. Where in Manhattan can French visitors see a statue of Joan of Arc?

A. At Riverside Drive and West Ninety-third Street.

Geography

Q. Why was the Old Stone Jug on Staten Island such a successful tavern for decades?

A. It was near Sailors' Snug Harbor, a retirement home for sailors.

Q. Running four and a half miles in the Bronx, the Grand Concourse was inspired by what thoroughfare in Europe?

A. The Champs-Élysées in Paris.

Q. Morrisania in the center of the Bronx is named for the family of what signer of the Declaration of Independence?

A. Lewis Morris.

Q. For whom is Seton Park in the North Bronx named?

A. A Scottish family loyal to Mary Stuart, queen of Scotland.

Q. What and where is Little Odessa?

A. The Russian community in the Brighton Beach section of Brooklyn.

Q. For what is Brighton Beach named?

A. Brighton, a historic resort in England.

Q. If you pass an open window and smell keittokirja (Finnish cabbage soup), you are probably in what part of Brooklyn with a large Scandinavian community?

A. Bay Ridge.

Geography

Q. What historic trek occurred in 1776 on Kings Highway in Brooklyn?

A. British troops under Lord Cornwallis marched to defeat Washington at the Battle of Long Island.

Q. Who resides on Riker's Island?

A. Inmates and staff of the New York City Penitentiary.

Q. What is the purpose of Potter's Field on Hart Island, part of the Bronx?

A. A free burial place for the destitute and unknown.

Q. Erected in 1902, a cross on Hart Island bears what inscription?

A. "He calleth His children by name."

Q. Early in the twentieth century, when upscale Roosevelt Island in the East River was Blackwell's Island, who resided there?

A. The insane, the destitute, and the imprisoned.

Q. For whom is Riis Park in Queens named?

A. Jacob Riis, a turn-of-the-century journalist and champion of the underdog.

Q. For whom is Fort Tryon Park in Upper Manhattan named?

A. William Tryon, the last British governor of New York.

GEOGRAPHY

Q. Frederick Law Olmstead, who designed Central and Prospect Parks, also designed what two thoroughfares in Brooklyn?

A. Eastern Parkway and Ocean Parkway.

Q. Who observed that "you can take a boy out of Brooklyn, but you can never get Brooklyn out of the boy"?

A. W. T. Ballard.

Q. On what Bronx street did women help retreating colonial soldiers by muffling the hoofbeats of their horses?

A. Featherbed Lane.

Q. Victory Boulevard on Staten Island commemorates what victory?

A. The Allies' victory over Germany in 1918.

Q. In 1997, the name of the Interboro Expressway between Queens and Brooklyn was changed to honor what local sports hero?

A. Jackie Robinson of the Brooklyn Dodgers.

Q. Where does a thoroughfare honor a local labor leader?

A. Harry Van Arsdale Jr. Boulevard in Queens.

Q. What New York skyscraper, once the world's tallest, was commissioned by a merchant who made his fortune in nickels and dimes?

A. The Woolworth Building, on Broadway between Barclay Street and Park Place.

GEOGRAPHY

Q. Better known as the Little Church Around the Corner, the Church of the Transfiguration on East Twenty-ninth Street is around the corner from what two avenues?

A. Fifth and Madison Avenues.

Q. More modest than its counterpart in Washington, D.C., the Vietnam Veterans Memorial Plaza is located where in Lower Manhattan?

A. At Water and Broad Streets.

Q. What area in Lower Manhattan is devoted to a reconstruction of early maritime and commercial activities?

A. South Street Seaport Historic District near Fulton and Pearl Streets.

Q. Brooklyn has how many thoroughfares named for saints?

A. Eleven.

Q. What has been New York's official sister city since 1960, and by how many miles are the urban siblings separated?

A. Tokyo, 10,870 miles.

Q. In what landmark district is Love Lane?

A. Brooklyn Heights.

Q. What Bronx thoroughfare is named for a Civil War officer who popularized a hairstyle for men?

A. Burnside Avenue, after Gen. Ambrose Burnside, who wore side whiskers that became known as "burnsides" and then "sideburns."

Geography

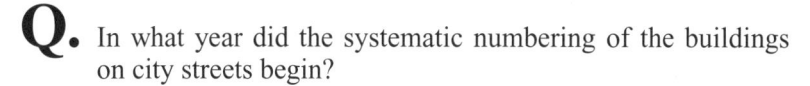

Q. In what year did the systematic numbering of the buildings on city streets begin?

A. 1793.

Q. In Washington Square Park can be found a statue of what great Italian hero?

A. Giuseppe Garibaldi.

Q. On May 4, 1897, what official signed the document legalizing the merger of the five boroughs into Greater New York?

A. New York State Governor Frank S. Black.

Q. Madison Avenue is the center of what industries?

A. Advertising and public relations.

Q. Texans with a sense of history will take off their six-gallon hats on what street in Lower Manhattan?

A. Houston Street, which is pronounced House-ton by New Yorkers.

Q. Where does a short street bear the name of Thomas Willett, the city's first mayor in 1665?

A. On the Lower East Side of Manhattan.

Q. Marco Polo, a Venetian trader in the thirteenth century, would have been at home in what two ethnic areas that adjoin in Lower Manhattan?

A. Little Italy and Chinatown.

GEOGRAPHY

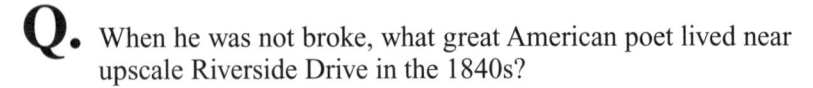

Q. When he was not broke, what great American poet lived near upscale Riverside Drive in the 1840s?

A. Edgar Allen Poe.

Q. Where can you buy a "fine preowned mink" or sable in New York City?

A. The Ritz, a thrift shop on West Fifty-seventh Street.

Q. What private park in Manhattan will not admit humans who do not live in the immediate area?

A. Gramercy Park on East Twentieth Street and Lexington Avenue.

Q. What body of water used to flow through Greenwich Village?

A. Minetta Brook.

Q. Gone by not forgotten by book lovers all over the world are the secondhand stores on what thoroughfare?

A. Fourth Avenue.

Q. When it is not stuck with traffic or closed for repair, what road links Long Island to Queens and Brooklyn and then links Brooklyn to the whole country?

A. The Belt Parkway.

GEOGRAPHY

WHERE TO GO IN NEW YORK

BARS
No one will think it unreasonable if you use the restroom before ordering a drink. So if you're going to get hassled, it'll be on your way out. One friend suggested tipping the bartender when you ask for the location of the restroom.

RESTAURANTS
I'd suggest looking for a serve-yourself, seat-yourself kind of place with a counter or salad bar. Pizza parlors are generally friendly. If there's a separate floor for eating, either upstairs or downstairs from the food-service area, there will often be restrooms there.

THEATERS AT INTERMISSION
Traditionally penniless drama students mingle with the sidewalk crowd at intermission and sneak in to see the second half of the play. If you time it right you can use this ploy to get in the restroom line.

ATRIUMS AND MALLS

WORLD FINANCIAL CENTER
West St.-Hudson R., Vesey-Liberty Sts.
Open 24 hours
In the Winter Garden facing semicircular marble steps: behind/under the steps, there's a semicircular arcade labeled "Winter Garden Gallery Shops." The women's room is on the right side, the men's room on the left. Leading north off the Winter Garden is "Courtyard Shops & Restaurants." More restrooms there.

EAST BROADWAY MALL
East Broadway (Market-Forsyth)
There are restrooms at the upstairs restaurant, Triple Eight Palace. Head back left, right, left.

HERALD CENTER
6th Ave. (33–34)
10–7 daily
Take express elevator to food court on 8th floor.

CRYSTAL PAVILION
805 3d Ave. (49-50). Entrances also on 3d Ave. and E. 50th St.
M-F 8 A.M.–10 or 11 P.M.; Sa 9–5
Go downstairs; facing the waterfall, restrooms are on the left.

OLYMPIC TOWER
E. 51st St. (5-Mad.); E. 52 St. (5-Mad.)
Daily 7 A.M.–midnight
The restrooms are just south of the public seating area, down a short curved corridor.

TRUMP TOWER
5th Ave. (56-57)
8 A.M.-10 P.M.
Walk to the back of the escalators to descend to the lower level. Follow the signs around left, then right. Restrooms angle off the same entrance.

PARK AVENUE PLAZA
55 E. 52 St. (Mad.-Park) Daily 8 A.M.–10 P.M.
There's an entrance also on E. 53d St. Just across from the waterfall is a drinking fountain and 2 private unisex toilets.

BOOKSTORES

STRAND
828 Broadway at 12th St.
M-Sa 9:30–9:30; Su 11–9:30
Women's room on left just past the stairs leading to basement; men's room around the corner from there. Check your bags.

MUSEUMS, GALLERIES & EXHIBITIONS

FORBES MAGAZINE GALLERIES
62 5th Ave. (12–12)
Tu-Sa 10–4
Restrooms are at entrance to the galleries, past the guards' desk, to the left.

NATIONAL ARTS CLUB
15 Gramercy Park (Gram. Pk. W.-Irving Pl.)
Daily 1–5
Gramercy Park is the continuation of E. 20th St. Go down the steps and jog right. The women's room is straight ahead; the men's room to the left of it.

STEINWAY HALL
109 W. 57th St. (6–7 Aves.)
M–W, F 9–6; Th 9–9; Sa 9–5; Su noon–5
The women's room, at front right of the piano showroom, is up two red-carpeted steps on left.

CARNEGIE HALL MUSEUM
154 W 57th St. (6–7 Aves.)
Daily 11–4:30
Admission free. Take stairs or elevator to 2d floor. Women's room back left, men's room back right.

MUSEUM OF AMERICAN ILLUSTRATORS
128 E. 63d St. (Park-Lex)
M, W–F 10–5; Tu 10–8
There's a unisex restroom on the lower level at back (3 steps up).

HOTELS

VISTA INTERNATIONAL HOTEL
3 World Trade Center (West & Liberty Sts.)
Enter through 1 World Trade Center. Go up the circular staircase. Restrooms are to the right, on the other side of the Vista Lounge.

ARLINGTON HOTEL
18 W. 25th St. (Bwy.-6th Ave.)
Go straight ahead—the unmarked, right-hand door in the back wall holds a tiny unisex restroom.

GEOGRAPHY

THE CARLTON
22 E. 29th St. (Mad.)
Turn left; the last door on the right leads downstairs.

SOUTHGATE TOWER HOTEL
371 7th Ave. (30–31)
Turn right before the gates leading to the elevators; follow the pictographs (including up a short flight of stairs).

ROGER WILLIAMS HOTEL
28 E. 31st St. (Mad.)
Restaurant hours: M–F 11:30 A.M.–10 P.M. Sa noon–10; Su closed
There's an entrance from the lobby into the corner restaurant, the Young Fu Noodle Shop. Restrooms are on your left.

SHERATON PARK AVENUE
Park Ave. (37)
Park Ave. entrance, turn left, past the lobby; restrooms are on the left. 37th St. entrance, go down corridor; restrooms on the right.

SHELBURNE HOTEL
303 Lexington Ave. (37-38)
Left then right.

DORAL PARK AVENUE HOTEL
90 Park Avenue (38)
Take elevator down to lower lobby. Turn right.

DORAL COURT HOTEL
130 E. 39th St. (Lex.)
A door labeled restrooms is just to the left of the desk.

DORAL TUSCANY HOTEL
E. 39 St. (Lex-Park)
Go right and then right again.

HELMSLEY HOTEL
212 W. 42d St. (2d–3d Aves.)
Look diagonally right—you'll see the restroom sign.

UN PLAZA HOTEL
E. 44th St. (1d-2d Aves.)
Go right, down the corridor to the elevators. Take one to the 2d floor. Go left off the elevators; women's room on left, men's room on right.

ROYALTON HOTEL
W. 44th St. (5–6 Aves.)
Restrooms are in an alcove along the wall on right, just before the food service counter. The women's room is very modern. Reportedly the men's room is even more spectacular.

THE ROOSEVELT HOTEL
E. 45th St. (Mad.-Vanderbilt Aves.)
Up stairs, turn right (up some more steps).

MARRIOTT MARQUIS HOTEL
1535 Broadway (45-46)
Enter on Broadway or W. 45 St. Restrooms on floors 6 & 7 are on the south side of the building. Restrooms on floors 3, 4, 5, 8, & 9 are on the north side.

MILFORD PLAZA HOTEL
8th Ave. (45–46)
The restrooms are on the ground floor, at back left, across from the entrance to the Stage Door Canteen and near the 46th St. entrance.

PARAMOUNT HOTEL
235 W. 46 St. (Bwy–8 Ave.)
Restrooms are on either side of the pay phones at back.

ROGER SMITH HOTEL
501 Lexington Ave. (47)
The women's room is at the top of the stairs to the left of the desk. Men's room: continue around the corner to the left.

EMBASSY SUITES HOTEL
1568 Broadway (47)
Take the elevator to the main lobby on the 3d floor. The restrooms are at back left.

HOTEL INTER-CONTINENTAL
111 E. 48th St. (Lex.-Park)
Women's room: Go straight ahead almost to the back counter, then turn right.

MARRIOTT EAST SIDE HOTEL
525 Lexington Ave. (48-49)
Turn right and go upstairs. Turn right and go up the steps or continue down corridor until you reach the Morgan D Conference Room on the left, and go right up the stairs there.

HOLIDAY INN CROWNE PLAZA
Broadway (48-49)
Take the escalator up to the lobby. Walk to the back of the escalators and turn left.

BEEKMAN TOWERS HOTEL
5 Mitchell Place (49 St. E. of 1st Ave.)
The attached restaurant at this orange brick art deco building is the Zephyr Grill. The restrooms are downstairs.

DORAL INN
541 Lexington Ave. (49–50)
Inside Gallery Bar, make a right, downstairs.

WALDORF-ASTORIA HOTEL
Park Ave. (49–50) There's also an entrance on Lex. Ave. (49–50 Streets).
From the Lex. side, take escalator up to lobby. From Park side, take stairs. Coming from Park, the men's room is on the left, women's room on the right.

HOTEL BEVERLY
125 W. 50 St. (Lex.)
Left up the stairs before the restaurant.

HELMSLEY PALACE
455 Mad. Ave. (50–51)
Enter through the courtyard. Restrooms are upstairs to the left. From the 50th & 51st St. entrances: go upstairs, right, up more stairs.

— 38 —

Geography

Loew's Summit
51st St. & Lexington Ave.
Restrooms on the mezzanine. Walk straight through the lobby—stairs to the mezzanine are on the left, across from the elevators. At the top of the stairs, turn left.

Omni Berkshire Place
E. 52d St. (Mad.-5th Aves.)
Entrance on 52d St., left halfway into lobby seating area.

Novotel Hotel
226 W. 52d St. (Bwy.–8th Ave.)
Take elevator up to lobby. Go pretty much straight ahead—there's a restroom sign on a square mirrored pillar. Then another sign will point you right.

New York Hilton
1335 6th Ave. (53d–54th)
Take escalator or elevator to the 2d-floor meeting rooms; restrooms are near the back on the 54th St. side.

Hotel Dorset
30 W. 54th St. (5th–6th Aves.)
To the back, then left.

Rihga Royal Hotel
151 W. 54th St. (6th–7th Aves.)
Enter Halcyon Restaurant. Go past the piano and head for the wine rack. The restrooms are behind it.

Ameritania Hotel
Broadway & 54th St.
Two narrow, unmarked doors on either side of a large potted plant.

St. Regis Hotel
2 E. 55th St. (5th Ave.)
Downstairs on left, right, down some more stairs, right to the end of the hall, left.

The Peninsula
700 5th Ave. (55)
Straight back (which, because of the architecture, means up and around). Both doorways lead to the same little foyer, off which are restrooms.

Omni Park Central
870 7th Ave. (55-56) There's another entrance on 56th St. (7th–Bwy.)
The way to the restrooms is clearly marked: left, then right.

The Drake Hotel
E. 56th St. (Park-Mad.)
Turn right at the desk, go past the elevators, down the stairs and follow the signs. Right.

Parker Meridien Hotel
118 W. 57th St. (6th–7th Aves.) There's also an entrance on 56th St.
Restrooms are down the stairs to left of Maurice Restaurant. The men's room is at the foot of the stairs; the women's room to the right of it.

Days Inn
440 W. 57th St. (9th–10th Aves.)
Go up a short flight of stairs and head toward the back.

Regency Hotel
540 Park Ave. (60–61)
Bear right, go down the hall toward the back.

Hotel Pierre
2 E. 61st St. (5th-Mad. Aves.)
Starting at the desk, make two rights, go up two wooden steps; the entrance is under the balcony on the right. The women's room is on the left; the men's room is on the right. (From the 5th Ave. entrance, the wooden steps are on the left.)

Mayflower Hotel
Central Park West (61)
Women's room: Turn right, make the first left; it's on the right. Men's room: Enter Conservatory Restaurant and make two rights.

Barbizon Hotel
140 E. 63d St. (Lex.)
The stairway to the mezzanine is accessible from both the lobby (E. 63d St.) and the Cafe (Lex. Ave.). Turn right at the top of the stairs.

Empire Hotel
W. 63d St. (Bwy.-Col.)
Go up the stairs and turn left. Women's room is on the right; men's room on the left, right by the end of the balcony.

Hotel Plaza Athenee
E. 64th St. (Mad.-Park)
Immediate left, walk to end of corridor, turn right.

Mayfair Regent Hotel
E. 65th St. (Park-Lex.)
Sharp right at foot of entrance stairs (entrance to Le Cirque).

The Westbury
E. 69th St. (Mad.)
If you use the 69th St. entrance, continue past the desk, through the farthest doorway (Fire Command Station). If you enter through The Polo on Madison (69–70) jog right, left (through the exit), then right.

Hotel Esplanade
305 West End Ave. (75-76)
The doorway (with the Max canopy) to the right of the main entrance will lead you to the back of the lobby where you will spot pictographs. Open the door, go downstairs and turn right.

Surrey Hotel
20 E. 76th St. (Mad.–Park Aves.)
They'll send you to the Pleiades Restaurant next door. Restrooms are on the right, past the bar.

GEOGRAPHY

HOTEL CARLYLE
Madison Ave. (76–77)
Bear left, down a few steps to the foyer. The restrooms are through a doorway diagonally left of you.

THE MARK
25 E. 77th (Mad.–5th Ave.)
Go up the circular stairway before the restaurant. At the top of the stairs, you'll see a restroom sign. Go down that corridor and turn left.

STANHOPE
995 5th Ave. (80–81)
Restrooms in alcove directly to the right of the desk.

EXCELSIOR HOTEL
45 W. 81st St. (CPW-Col.)
This small hotel sends you to the attached coffee shop; there's an unmarked restroom in back, on left.

LIBRARIES

MID-MANHATTAN LIBRARY
455 5th Ave. (39–40)
M & W 9–9; Tu & Th 11–7; F & Sa 10–6
Restroom across from and to left of the stairway on the 2d–5th floors.

NEW YORK PUBLIC LIBRARY
5th Ave. (40–42)
Tu–W 11–7:30; Th–Sa 10–6
Women's room—inside 42d St. entrance, ground floor & 3d floor; men's room—3d floor.

PARKS & PLAYGROUNDS

BATTERY PARK/CASTLE CLINTON
N. end of Battery Park
8:30-5 P.M., year-round
Restrooms are within castle walls, and in stone building elsewhere in park: at north end, across from WUI Plaza; at south end, next to playground.

WASHINGTON SQUARE PARK
Washington Sq. S. (Thompson St.)
7 A.M.–10 P.M.
Stone building on Wash. Sq. South (halfway along). No toilet seats but they have paper.

REFRESHMENT STAND/CENTRAL PARK
67th St., mid-park
Restrooms are on the west side of the snack bar.

LOEB BOATHOUSE/CENTRAL PARK
75th St., mid-park
Restrooms are on the east side of the boathouse.

RELIGIOUS BUILDINGS

TRINITY CHURCH
Bwy. & Wall St.
M–F 7–6; Sa & Su 8–4
In the back, on the right.

TEMPLE EMANU-EL
1 E. 65th St. (5th Ave.)
Daily 10–5
The sanctuary is to the left, the gift shop is to the right. Just across from the gift shop is a glass door leading downstairs to the restrooms.

CATHEDRAL CHURCH OF ST. JOHN THE DIVINE
Amsterdam Ave. (112)
Daily 7–5
Restrooms are in back of the gift shop, which is about two-thirds of the way into the cathedral, on the left. There are also restrooms downstairs: women take stairs on right, men bear left, both down long corridors.

RIVERSIDE CHURCH
Riverside Dr.-Claremont Ave., 120th–122d Sts.
M–Sa 9 A.M.–10 P.M.; Su 8:30 A.M.–5 P.M.
Enter at Claremont Ave. and what would be W. 121st St. There are restroom signs by the visitors' desk: men's room is nearby, women's room is down the hall.

SIGHTSEEING

UNITED NATIONS
1st Ave. (45–46)
M–F 9–5; Sa, Su & Holidays 9:15–5
Walk through metal detectors, then take elevator to the left of the information desk or the stairway to right. On the lower level, the women's room is to the left, the men's room is ahead and to the right.

ROCKEFELLER CENTER
5th–6th Aves., W. 49th–51st Sts.
M–F 7 A.M.–7 P.M.; Sa & Su 10–6
If entering at 630 5th Ave. (50–51), go downstairs, bear left, go down marble stairs/ramp, and bear right alongside the American Festival Cafe. Head right past the newsstand and bazaar shop—the restrooms are in that corridor.

PLACES YOU'D THINK WOULD HAVE PUBLIC RESTROOMS BUT DON'T

The Empire State Building
St. Patrick's Cathedral
The Woolworth Building
Tower Records
Unification Church HQ (at Hotel New Yorker)

Excerpted from WHERE TO GO: A GUIDE TO MANHATTAN'S TOILETS by Vicki Rovere, used by permission of the author. For more information, contact Vicki Rovere at 339 Lafayette St., New York, NY 10012.

ENTERTAINMENT
CHAPTER TWO

What a caterwauling do you keep here!
—Shakespeare, *Twelfth Night*

Q. What are the three "Mets" in New York City?

A. The Metropolitan Museum of Art, the Metropolitan Opera, and the Mets, the baseball team.

Q. What was the world's first movie theater?

A. Holland Brothers Kinetoscope Parlor, which opened in 1894.

Q. When was the first radio broadcast from the Metropolitan Opera?

A. 1910.

Q. What was the name of the naive New York visitor played by James Stewart in a 1936 Frank Capra film?

A. Mr. Longfellow Deeds in *Mr. Deeds Goes to Town*.

Q. Who, in New York on November 11, 1817, gave the nation's first exhibition of sword swallowing?

A. Senaa Samma of India.

ENTERTAINMENT

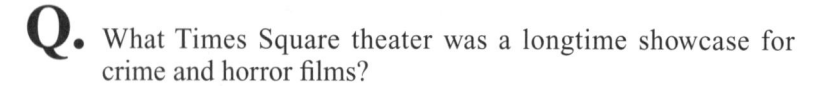

Q. What Times Square theater was a longtime showcase for crime and horror films?

A. The Rialto.

Q. The first crossword puzzle appeared on December 21, 1913, on the pages of what newspaper?

A. The *New York World*.

Q. Who was the longtime editor of the *New York Times* crossword puzzle, one of the toughest puzzles in the country?

A. Margaret P. Farrar, from 1942 to 1969.

Q. What was the first full-length talking picture?

A. *Lights of New York,* which opened with a gala performance on July 6, 1928, at the Strand Theater in Times Square.

Q. In the middle of the twentieth century, you were not a real celebrity until a sandwich was named for you in what restaurant?

A. Reuben's, which was on East Fifty-eighth Street near Fifth Avenue.

Q. What was George M. Cohan's nostalgic love song to the city?

A. "Give My Regards to Broadway."

Q. On television, the playmate of Lamb Chop, Hush Puppy, and other puppets is what Bronxite?

A. Shari Lewis.

Times Square, originally occupied by livery stables and harness makers, and a longtime center of sleaze, is now experiencing a rebirth anchored by Disney's multi-million-dollar restoration of the New Amsterdam Theater. New York Convention and Visitors Bureau.

ENTERTAINMENT

Q. What "man from U.N.C.L.E." was really from New York?

A. Robert Vaughn.

Q. When did legendary French actress Sarah Bernhardt make her debut in New York?

A. November 8, 1880.

Q. In the 1930s, Minsky's Theater was world famous for what form of risqué entertainment that seems tame by current standards of morality?

A. Burlesque.

Q. What performer at Minsky's Theater was famous for her fan dance?

A. Sally Rand.

Q. When did the first circus arrive in the town of New York?

A. In 1795, New Yorkers enjoyed Rickett's Circus from England.

Q. On the night President Lincoln was assassinated at Ford's Theater in Washington, he was watching a play starring what popular New York actress?

A. Laura Keene.

Q. When it opened on Broadway in 1835, what was the billing of the world's first flea circus?

A. Extraordinary Exhibition of the Industrious Fleas.

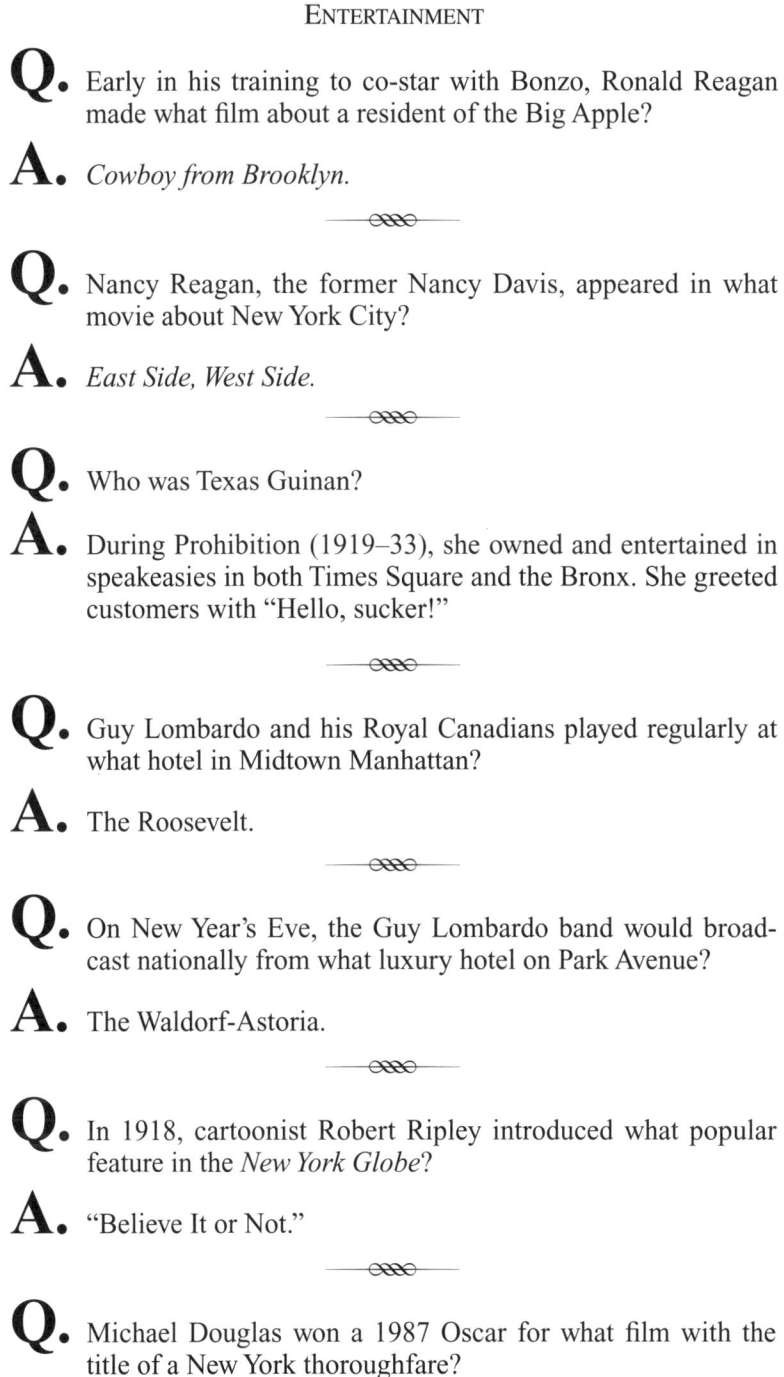

Entertainment

Q. Early in his training to co-star with Bonzo, Ronald Reagan made what film about a resident of the Big Apple?

A. *Cowboy from Brooklyn.*

Q. Nancy Reagan, the former Nancy Davis, appeared in what movie about New York City?

A. *East Side, West Side.*

Q. Who was Texas Guinan?

A. During Prohibition (1919–33), she owned and entertained in speakeasies in both Times Square and the Bronx. She greeted customers with "Hello, sucker!"

Q. Guy Lombardo and his Royal Canadians played regularly at what hotel in Midtown Manhattan?

A. The Roosevelt.

Q. On New Year's Eve, the Guy Lombardo band would broadcast nationally from what luxury hotel on Park Avenue?

A. The Waldorf-Astoria.

Q. In 1918, cartoonist Robert Ripley introduced what popular feature in the *New York Globe*?

A. "Believe It or Not."

Q. Michael Douglas won a 1987 Oscar for what film with the title of a New York thoroughfare?

A. *Wall Street.*

ENTERTAINMENT

Q. The Broadway musical *Show Boat,* about the famous Mississippi *Cotton Blossom,* was written in 1927 by what two New Yorkers?

A. Jerome Kern and Oscar Hammerstein II.

Q. What was the name of the tumultuous 1926 movie with Greta Garbo and Manhattan's Ricardo Cortez?

A. *The Torrent.*

Q. What New Yorker immortalized a restaurant owned by Alice May Brock in a song?

A. Arlo Guthrie.

Q. In what early film did John Wayne play a New York office worker who had to contend with a ruthless woman instead of his usual Apaches or rustlers?

A. *Baby Face* in 1933. Barbara Stanwyck played the woman.

Q. In the movie *The Silence of the Lambs,* a cannibal named Hannibal pursued a character played by what New Yorker?

A. Jodie Foster.

Q. When Latin band leader Xavier Cugat needed a singer for his sambas and rhumbas, what Brooklyn señorita did he hire and later marry?

A. Abbe Lane.

Q. After an opening night on Broadway, at what eatery does the cast await the newspaper reviews?

A. Sardi's at 234 West Forty-fourth Street.

ENTERTAINMENT

Q. What famous Manhattan restaurant began during Prohibition as a speakeasy?

A. 21, located, of course, at 21 West Fifty-second Street.

Q. The 21's famous burgers contain what ingredients?

A. Ground sirloin, bread crumbs, celery, nutmeg, and Worcestershire sauce.

Q. John Travolta hung out at what Brooklyn disco in the movie *Saturday Night Fever*?

A. 2001 Odyssey.

Q. On public radio station WNYC, who began to feature folk songs and country music in 1945?

A. Oscar Brand.

Q. What is New York City's public television station?

A. WNET, Channel 13.

Q. Jazz lover Barney Josephson established what nightclub in Greenwich Village?

A. Café Society.

Q. Lovers of folk music and stand-up comedy frequented what Greenwich Village nightclub founded by Max Gordon?

A. Village Vanguard.

ENTERTAINMENT

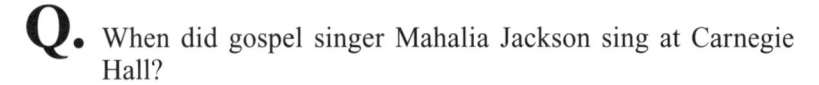

Q. When did gospel singer Mahalia Jackson sing at Carnegie Hall?

A. October 4, 1950.

Q. What African-American ballet dancer became the founder and director of the Dance Theater of Harlem?

A. Arthur Mitchell.

Q. In what film did Arnold Schwarzenegger play an ancient Greek hero who gets involved with modern-day wrestlers and gangsters in New York?

A. *Hercules in New York.*

Q. Cher and Nicholas Cage stared at the sky over Brooklyn in what film?

A. *Moonstruck.*

Q. In what film about Queens did a New York cop played by Nicholas Cage share his lottery winnings with a waitress played by Bridget Fonda?

A. *It Could Happen to You.*

Q. Long before Sunday talk shows on television, Town Hall in Manhattan was the site of what radio series devoted to national and world events?

A. *America's Town Meeting of the Air.*

Q. What mild-mannered New Yorker played a mild-mannered superhero in a succession of blockbuster films?

A. Christopher Reeve.

ENTERTAINMENT

Q. In what church did Martha Graham and Isadora Duncan dance as well as pray?

A. St. Mark's Church in-the-Bowery.

Q. A Pulitzer Prize was awarded to what musical about what great and unique mayor of New York?

A. *Fiorello!* It is about Fiorello LaGuardia.

Q. Best known for directing *Birth of a Nation,* David Wark Griffith was equally proud of what film about New York?

A. *The Struggle.*

Q. New York's drop in crime during the mid-1990s may or may not be due to the impact of what two top-rated television shows about local crime and punishment?

A. *Law and Order* and *NYPD Blue.*

Q. John Lennon fans can offer their respects to his memory at what quiet place?

A. Strawberry Fields in Central Park near West Seventy-second Street.

Q. How did Met tenor Enrico Caruso show his appreciation for the food and service at Yonah Schimmel's knishery?

A. He drew one of his famous self-portrait caricatures for display on a wall.

Q. On May 1, 1967, Priscilla Beaulieu, a belle from Brooklyn, married what rock star from the Deep South?

A. Elvis Presley.

ENTERTAINMENT

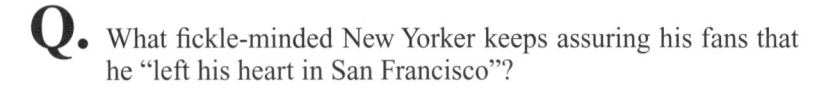

Q. What fickle-minded New Yorker keeps assuring his fans that he "left his heart in San Francisco"?

A. Tony Bennett.

Q. How did Samuel Joseph Mostel get the nickname Zero?

A. He says it was his score on an IQ test in school.

Q. What movie sleuths proved that crime does not pay in New York—at least, while they were in town?

A. Nick Charles, Sherlock Holmes, Charlie Chan, Ellery Queen, Nero Wolfe, Mike Shayne, and Philo Vance.

Q. Marilyn Monroe was married to what dramatist from Brooklyn?

A. Arthur Miller.

Q. Bela Lugosi never won an Oscar for playing Dracula, but what New Yorker won a 1994 Oscar for playing Lugosi?

A. Martin Landau.

Q. In what long-running play did Boris Karloff play a Brooklynite?

A. *Arsenic and Old Lace.*

Q. Which of New York's famous women appeared in *Golden Girls* on television?

A. Bea Arthur and Estelle Getty.

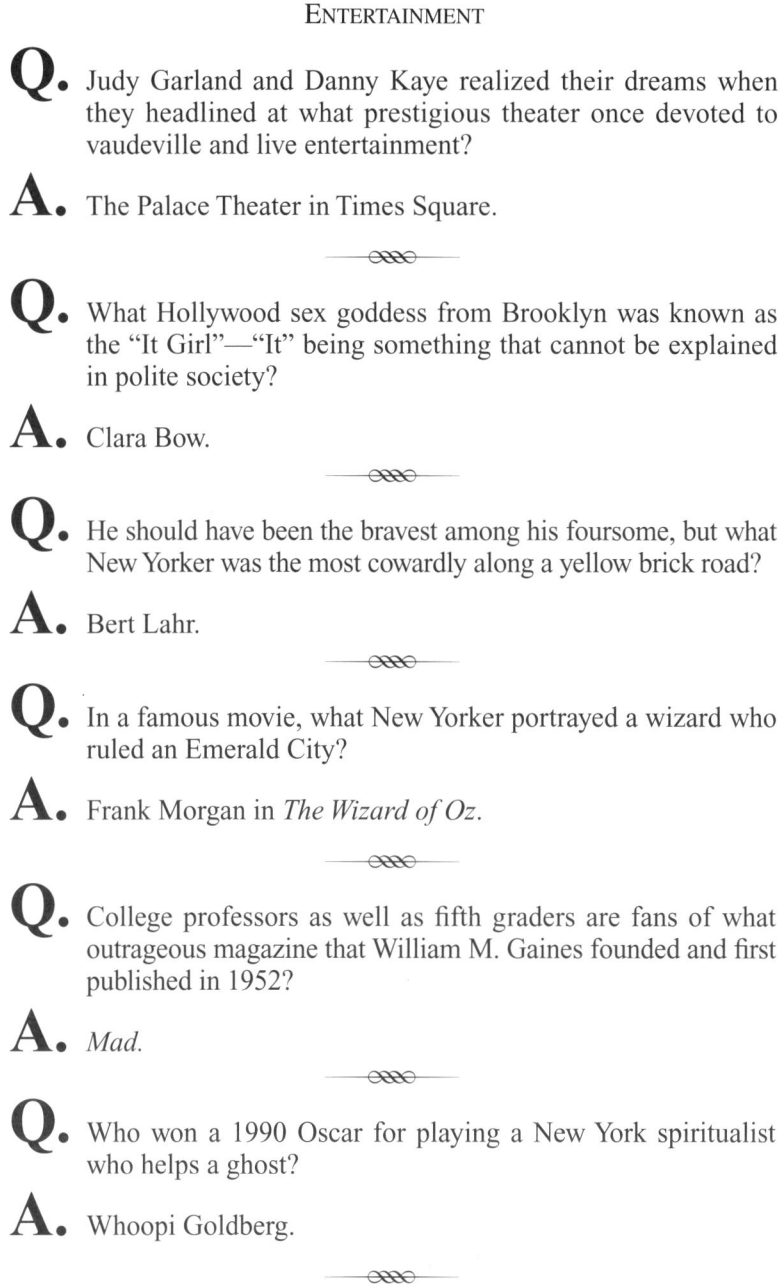

ENTERTAINMENT

Q. Judy Garland and Danny Kaye realized their dreams when they headlined at what prestigious theater once devoted to vaudeville and live entertainment?

A. The Palace Theater in Times Square.

Q. What Hollywood sex goddess from Brooklyn was known as the "It Girl"—"It" being something that cannot be explained in polite society?

A. Clara Bow.

Q. He should have been the bravest among his foursome, but what New Yorker was the most cowardly along a yellow brick road?

A. Bert Lahr.

Q. In a famous movie, what New Yorker portrayed a wizard who ruled an Emerald City?

A. Frank Morgan in *The Wizard of Oz*.

Q. College professors as well as fifth graders are fans of what outrageous magazine that William M. Gaines founded and first published in 1952?

A. *Mad.*

Q. Who won a 1990 Oscar for playing a New York spiritualist who helps a ghost?

A. Whoopi Goldberg.

Q. In a popular television series, who plays a Los Angeles detective who never cleans his raincoat and never appears with his wife?

A. Peter Falk of *Columbo*.

— 51 —

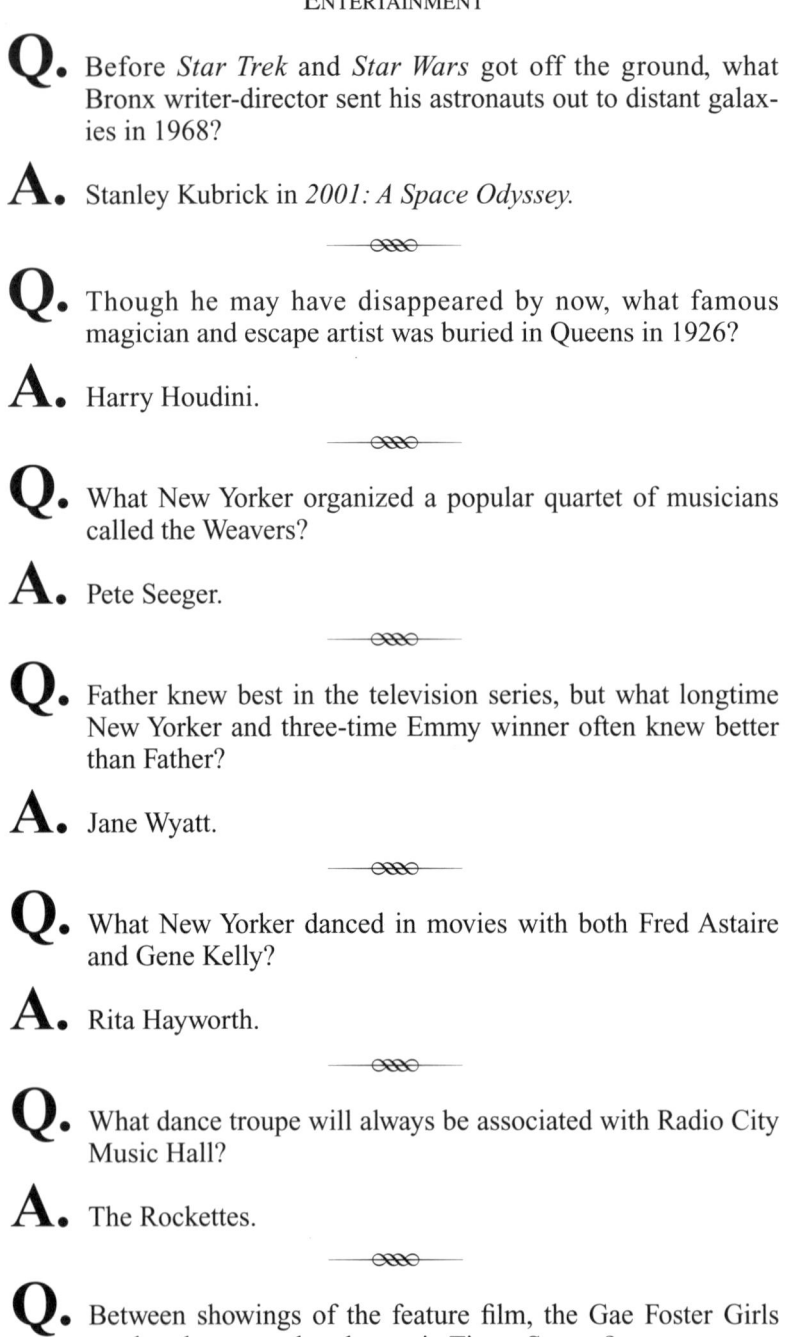

ENTERTAINMENT

Q. Before *Star Trek* and *Star Wars* got off the ground, what Bronx writer-director sent his astronauts out to distant galaxies in 1968?

A. Stanley Kubrick in *2001: A Space Odyssey.*

Q. Though he may have disappeared by now, what famous magician and escape artist was buried in Queens in 1926?

A. Harry Houdini.

Q. What New Yorker organized a popular quartet of musicians called the Weavers?

A. Pete Seeger.

Q. Father knew best in the television series, but what longtime New Yorker and three-time Emmy winner often knew better than Father?

A. Jane Wyatt.

Q. What New Yorker danced in movies with both Fred Astaire and Gene Kelly?

A. Rita Hayworth.

Q. What dance troupe will always be associated with Radio City Music Hall?

A. The Rockettes.

Q. Between showings of the feature film, the Gae Foster Girls used to dance at what theater in Times Square?

A. The Roxy.

ENTERTAINMENT

Q. What Brooklynite directed the movie *Manhattan*?

A. Woody Allen.

Q. In a series of popular films, what New Yorker wrote about and portrayed a guy from Philadelphia who was often down and groggy but never completely out?

A. Sylvester Stallone in the Rocky movies.

Q. In maybe the greatest of all screen duels, what New Yorker crossed sabers with Ronald Colman in *The Prisoner of Zenda*?

A. Douglas Fairbanks Jr.

Q. Academy Award-winner Claudette Colbert attended what Manhattan public school that was famous for training secretaries rather than actors?

A. Washington Irving High School for Girls.

Q. What was Marlon Brando's alma mater in New York?

A. The Actors Studio.

Q. Whose father once owned the Latin Quarter, a famous nightclub?

A. Television personality Barbara Walters.

Q. Supershowman Billy Rose operated what spectacular nightclub in the 1930s?

A. The Casa Mañana.

ON THE BOW'RY, THE BOW'RY! I'LL NEVER GO THERE ANY MORE!

Though it is named after the Dutch word for *farm*, the Bowery, a short street, less than a mile long, in Lower Manhattan, evokes degradation rather than vegetation. The original farm belonged to Peter Stuyvesant, governor of New Amsterdam from 1647 to 1664. Rather than build a new path from the farm to his office near the Battery, Stuyvesant did the cost-effective thing and appropriated the path that the Algonquin tribe had used to visit their Dutch neighbors. When the Thirteen Colonies began their war for independence from England in 1776, the former Indian path known as the Bowery was part of a royal highway to New England and the site of frequent skirmishes for its control.

By the 1820s, the surrounding area was no longer devoted to farming but to housing newcomers who arrived destitute from Europe, seeking their fortune in the New World. Once they had saved enough money by working as servants and day laborers, many of the immigrants moved on to farms and cities across the country. Others remained in town, fanning out to create Little Italy, Little Germany, and the medley of ethnic neighborhoods that became known as the Lower East Side. The Bowery itself became a recreational and theatrical center and the site of the first stage production of *Uncle Tom's Cabin* in 1852 at the Great Bowery Theater. Because poor and unsophisticated immigrants were not welcome at the Broadway establishments of the gentry, the Bowery became a street of affordable saloons, dance halls, brothels, gambling rooms, and flophouses. Stephen Foster, America's Minstrel and composer of such beloved songs as "My Old Kentucky Home," lived in a twenty-cent-a-night flophouse on the Bowery in 1864. Later in the century, another Bowery resident was Stephen Crane, author of *Maggie: A Girl of the Streets* and *The Red Badge of Courage*.

By 1891, the Bowery was so firmly established as the country's Skid Row that Charles M. Hoyt wrote a song about it. Few people remember the songs about the New York Stock Exchange and the Brooklyn Bridge, but almost everyone knows "The Bow'ry" and the immortal refrain, "The Bow'ry, The Bow'ry / They say such things and they do such things / On the Bow'ry, the Bow'ry / I'll never go there any more!"

The Bowery's permanent population of flophouse and doorway dwellers remained sizable and stable until the early 1940s, when jobs for the unskilled were created during World War II, and Franklin D. Roosevelt's New Deal of social and economic safety nets began to kick in, providing government and hometown assistance for people who needed help.

Thanks to the Bowery Mission and the Volunteers of America, established in 1879 and 1896 respectively, the homeless men and women who still come to the Bowery are fed, clothed, and treated for medical problems. Once returned to physical health, they are offered spiritual and emotional guidance that can restore them to their families and into society.

ENTERTAINMENT

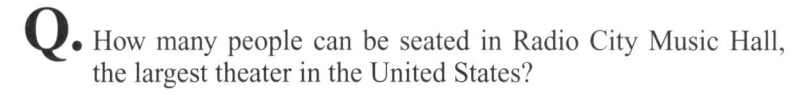

Q. How many people can be seated in Radio City Music Hall, the largest theater in the United States?

A. Six thousand.

Q. In 1941, what New Yorker stunned movie fans all over the world when she replaced Jeanette MacDonald as Nelson Eddy's singing partner?

A. Risë Stevens, a star of the Metropolitan Opera.

Q. What, appropriately, was the first play at the Bowery Theater in 1826?

A. *The Road to Ruin.*

Q. What actress-singer from the Bronx ran the economic gamut from a welfare mother in the film *Claudine* to a business tycoon in the television series *Dynasty*?

A. Diahann Carroll.

Q. In what film did a Russian defector played by Robin Williams find friends but no bargains in what upscale Manhattan department store?

A. *Moscow on the Hudson,* at Bloomingdale's.

Q. The movie *New York, New York* was made by what two New Yorkers?

A. Director Martin Scorsese and actor Robert De Niro.

Q. Before singing about love in the South Pacific, Mary Martin sang "Love in Bloom" in what movie about New York?

A. *New York Town.*

ENTERTAINMENT

Q. What Bronxite, once a sixth-grade teacher, formed a rock band popular in the late 1970s and again in the late 1990s?

A. Gene Simmons of Kiss.

Q. In what film, made during the Great Depression, did the character played by Ginger Rogers learn the important truth that a poor girl can be much happier than an heiress?

A. *Fifth Avenue Girl.*

Q. When he ran away from his East Harlem home at sixteen, what was the ambition of future Academy Award-winner Burt Lancaster?

A. To become a circus acrobat.

Q. Theater has not been the same since Ellen Stewart started what innovative production center in 1961?

A. La Mama.

Q. Where was the original production of *Hair* in 1967?

A. At Joseph Papp's Public Theater on Lafayette Street.

Q. Where in New York will you eventually see all thirty-eight of Shakespeare's plays—and for free?

A. The Delacorte Theater in Central Park.

Q. Who established the free Delacorte Theater in Central Park?

A. George T. Delacorte, owner of the Dell Publishing Company.

ENTERTAINMENT

Q. Whether they are Democrats or Republicans, ambitious politicians have to pass inspection by what radio interviewer from Brooklyn?

A. Larry King.

Q. Outside what apartment building at 1 West Seventy-second Street was John Lennon killed?

A. The Dakota.

Q. In what movie does a newborn take up residence at the Dakota Apartments across the street from Central Park?

A. *Rosemary's Baby.*

Q. Paul Mazursky, from the disenchanted borough of Brooklyn, has directed a modern version of what Shakespeare play about an enchanted island?

A. *The Tempest.*

Q. The *Star Wars* trilogy might not have had a happy ending without Lando Calrissian who was played by what savvy New Yorker?

A. Billy Dee Williams.

Q. For what product did operatic superstar Beverly Sills sing a radio commercial in her youth?

A. Rinso.

Q. Born in a tough Brooklyn neighborhood, who had no trouble winning an Oscar for whipping Richard Gere into an officer and a gentleman?

A. Lou Gossett Jr.

ENTERTAINMENT

Q. The title role in *King of New York* was played by what actor from Queens?

A. Christopher Walken.

Q. In the Alfred Hitchcock thriller *North by Northwest*, the antagonists begin their pursuit of Cary Grant at what usually restful hotel?

A. The Plaza.

Q. To what New York hotel did President and Mrs. Clinton take Chelsea for her seventeenth birthday?

A. The Waldorf-Astoria.

Q. What Brooklyn actor is as proud of his early work in Shakespeare as in his Emmy-winning role as a tough detective on television?

A. Jimmy Smits of *NYPD Blue*.

Q. Marlon Brando won an Oscar in 1954 for his role as a worker in what peripheral part of Manhattan?

A. *On the Waterfront.*

Q. What three vastly popular comedy teams were composed of New Yorkers?

A. The Marx Brothers, the Ritz Brothers, and the Three Stooges.

Q. By the time he died in 1981, what entertainer from the Lower East Side had become such a popular emcee that he was called Toastmaster General of the United States?

A. George Jessel.

ENTERTAINMENT

Q. When it comes to tell-all television, what New Yorker gained a reputation for his show's uninhibited guests?

A. Geraldo Rivera.

Q. What Brooklyn movie actor was most acclaimed for portraying Native Americans, especially Apache Chief Cochise, whom he played three times?

A. Jeff Chandler.

Q. What versatile actor disguised his New York accent to play a Tibetan high lama in *Lost Horizon*?

A. Sam Jaffe.

Q. Flatbush in Brooklyn was the site of Wild West scenes in what most thrilling movie serial of all time?

A. *The Perils of Pauline.*

Q. How did comedian Jimmy Durante describe himself?

A. "Dere's a million good-lookin' guys, but I'm a novelty."

Q. What are the ingredients of a Manhattan cocktail?

A. Four parts whiskey, one part dry vermouth, and a dash of bitters.

Q. People who do not like their orange juice straight may want to mix a Bronx cocktail, which includes what two additional ingredients?

A. Gin and vermouth.

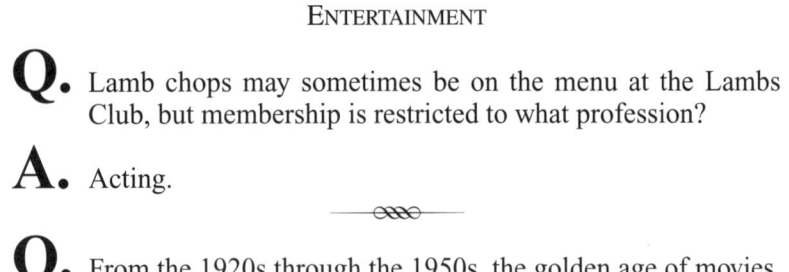

Q. Lamb chops may sometimes be on the menu at the Lambs Club, but membership is restricted to what profession?

A. Acting.

Q. From the 1920s through the 1950s, the golden age of movies, what were the two big theater chains in the city?

A. Loew's and RKO.

Q. Jimmy Walker, elected mayor in 1925, had written what great love song that appealed to older voters?

A. "Will You Love Me in December as You Did in May?"

Q. Early in the twentieth century, who were the members of the royal family of Broadway?

A. Ethel, Lionel, and John Barrymore.

Q. In a long-running play and film, who came to dinner and outstayed his welcome?

A. Monty Woolley in *The Man Who Came to Dinner*.

Q. Former bootlegger Sherman Billingsley was the owner of what exclusive nightclub?

A. The Stork Club.

Q. Though he had attended three excellent schools—City College, Cooper Union, and Columbia University—what Broadway actor excelled as an ignorant lowlife in *Tobacco Road*?

A. Henry Hull.

ENTERTAINMENT

Q. What was the achievement of New Yorker Marcus Loew?

A. In addition to owning a chain of movie theaters, he controlled the MGM film studio.

Q. What New Yorker was the chief of production at MGM?

A. Irving Thalberg.

Q. What New York actress has played a Manhattan mistress, a cop in Brooklyn, and a working girl from Staten Island?

A. Melanie Griffith.

Q. Some lovers come together from opposite ends of the earth, but what two stars came together from opposite ends of New York?

A. Bronxite Anne Bancroft and Brooklynite Mel Brooks.

Q. In what film set in New York did Sir Laurence Olivier play a Nazi killer on the run?

A. *Marathon Man.*

Q. Sir Ralph Richardson portrayed an upscale New York doctor in what film?

A. *Washington Square.*

Q. Sir John Gielgud won an Oscar for playing a valet in what film about a thirsty New York millionaire?

A. *Arthur.*

Entertainment

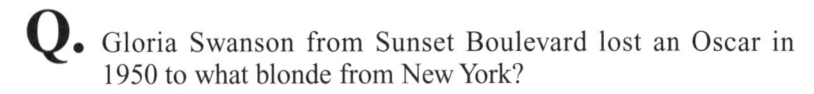

Q. Gloria Swanson from Sunset Boulevard lost an Oscar in 1950 to what blonde from New York?

A. Judy Holliday.

Q. Though she was acclaimed for *Evita,* many of Madonna's fans preferred her as an East Village hippie in what earlier film?

A. *Desperately Seeking Susan.*

Q. Newsperson Donna Hanover, wife of Mayor Rudolph Giuliani, appeared in what film about an unconventional publisher?

A. *The People vs. Larry Flynt.*

Q. Since what year has Bobby Short been performing the golden oldies of Gershwin and Cole Porter at the luxurious Café Carlyle on the Upper East Side?

A. 1968.

Q. What opera by George Gershwin opened in New York on October 10, 1935?

A. *Porgy and Bess.*

Q. In 1937, what was the hit Broadway musical sponsored by the International Ladies Garment Workers Union?

A. *Pins and Needles.*

Q. Transmitted in 1941 on WNBT in New York, the first television commercial featured what product?

A. Bulova watches.

ENTERTAINMENT

Manhattan

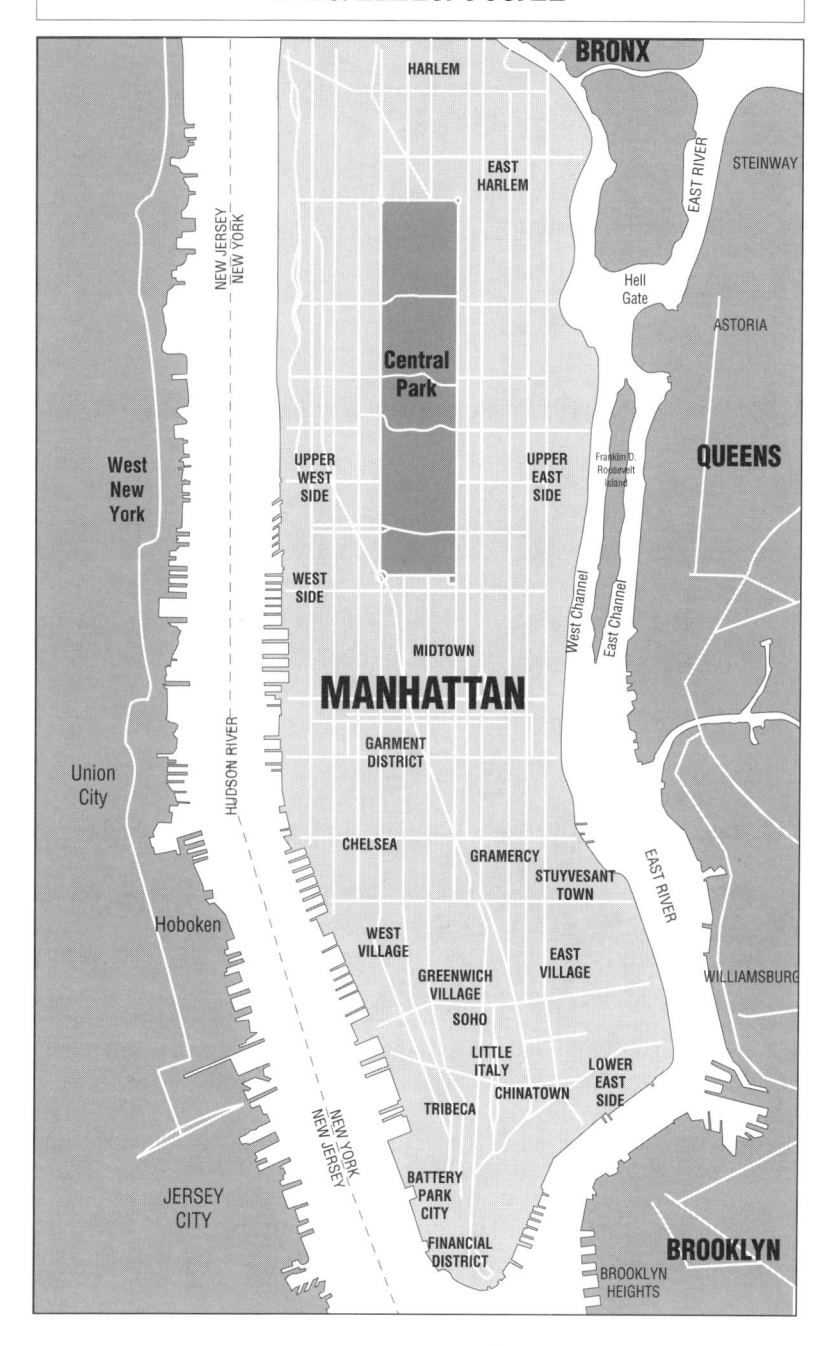

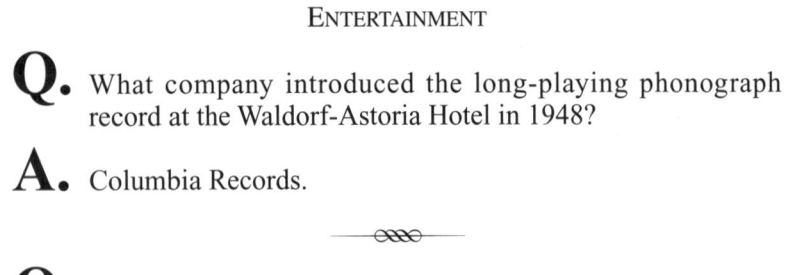

ENTERTAINMENT

Q. What company introduced the long-playing phonograph record at the Waldorf-Astoria Hotel in 1948?

A. Columbia Records.

Q. In what film did rugged Texan Tommy Lee Jones play a gentle New York priest?

A. *Broken Vows.*

Q. Who won a 1955 Oscar for playing Marty, a shy butcher from the Bronx?

A. Ernest Borgnine.

Q. In what film did a New York cop played by Gene Hackman pursue drug smugglers from abroad?

A. *The French Connection.*

Q. *The French Connection* was based on the experiences of what real-life detective?

A. Eddie Egan.

Q. What Harlem theater is associated with great jazz musicians?

A. The Apollo.

Q. Cab Calloway and Duke Ellington appeared frequently in what Harlem nightclub?

A. The Cotton Club.

ENTERTAINMENT

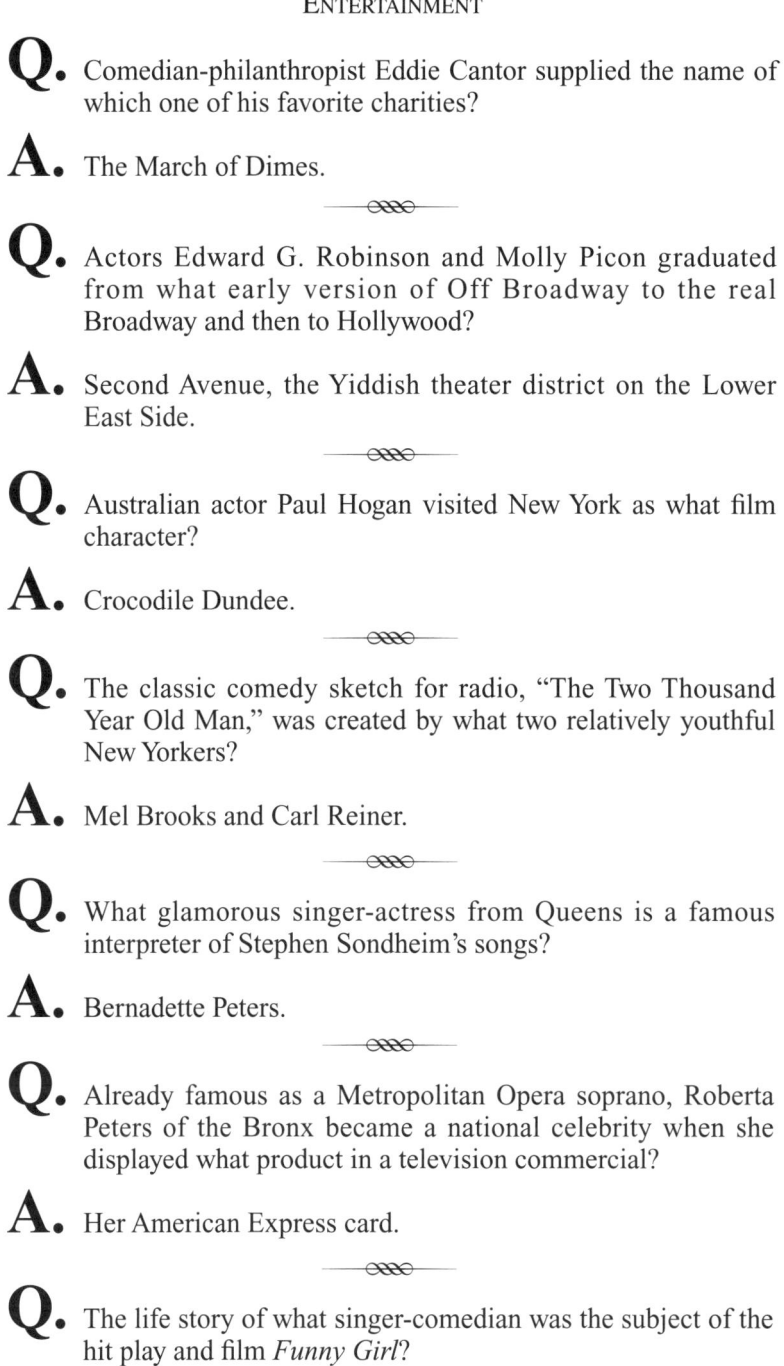

Q. Comedian-philanthropist Eddie Cantor supplied the name of which one of his favorite charities?

A. The March of Dimes.

Q. Actors Edward G. Robinson and Molly Picon graduated from what early version of Off Broadway to the real Broadway and then to Hollywood?

A. Second Avenue, the Yiddish theater district on the Lower East Side.

Q. Australian actor Paul Hogan visited New York as what film character?

A. Crocodile Dundee.

Q. The classic comedy sketch for radio, "The Two Thousand Year Old Man," was created by what two relatively youthful New Yorkers?

A. Mel Brooks and Carl Reiner.

Q. What glamorous singer-actress from Queens is a famous interpreter of Stephen Sondheim's songs?

A. Bernadette Peters.

Q. Already famous as a Metropolitan Opera soprano, Roberta Peters of the Bronx became a national celebrity when she displayed what product in a television commercial?

A. Her American Express card.

Q. The life story of what singer-comedian was the subject of the hit play and film *Funny Girl*?

A. Fanny Brice.

ENTERTAINMENT

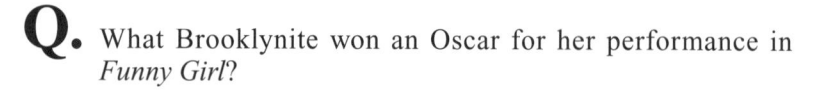

Q. What Brooklynite won an Oscar for her performance in *Funny Girl*?

A. Barbra Streisand.

Q. He is now a top director, but as an actor in *All in the Family*, what was the nickname of Rob Reiner?

A. Meathead.

Q. In what play did Sammy Davis Jr. become a Broadway star?

A. *Mr. Wonderful.*

Q. Who succeeded in winning a 1995 Tony after playing in *How to Succeed in Business Without Really Trying* on Broadway?

A. Matthew Broderick.

Q. What Brooklynite played a vampire in a movie about his own borough?

A. Eddie Murphy.

Q. A couple of Brooklyn plumbers get involved with lizard-humans from Dinohattan in what film?

A. *Super Mario Brothers.*

Q. *Dead Man Walking* was directed by what longtime resident of Greenwich Village?

A. Tim Robbins.

ENTERTAINMENT

Q. What rival "gansta" rappers from New York were killed within six months of each other in Los Angeles?

A. Tupac Shakur and Christopher G. Wallace, aka Notorious B.I.G.

Q. What New York director has been accused of rewriting history with his movies about presidents?

A. Oliver Stone.

Q. In what film did Jesus and flower children visit New York?

A. *Godspell*.

Q. Where is Schubert Alley, the legendary heart of the Broadway theater district?

A. From West Forty-fourth to West Forty-fifth streets, between Broadway and Eighth Avenue.

Q. In 1932, what was the world's first hotel to install television?

A. The New Yorker, but only in the expensive rooms.

Q. What popular dances originated at the Savoy Ballroom in Harlem?

A. Lindy Hop and Susie Q.

Q. What talk-show host and disc jockey has been leading local radio and television fans down memory lane for almost half a century?

A. Joe Franklin.

ENTERTAINMENT

An aerial view of Lower Manhattan, the site of the original Dutch settlement, shows today's Financial District and Battery Park on the southern tip of Manhattan. New York Convention and Visitors Bureau.

Q. What two New Yorkers were among *The Lords of Flatbush* in the film by that name?

A. Henry Winkler and Sylvester Stallone.

Q. What Bronxite was as famous for his evil Iago in Shakespeare's *Othello* as for his Curly, a handsome cowboy in the musical *Oklahoma*?

A. Alfred Drake.

Q. A Brooklyn pizza joint caused a riot in what hit film?

A. Spike Lee's *Do the Right Thing*.

Q. Robert Redford studied at what school in Brooklyn?

A. Pratt Institute.

Q. Who were the Copasetics?

A. A group of tap dancers in the 1970s from Queens.

ENTERTAINMENT

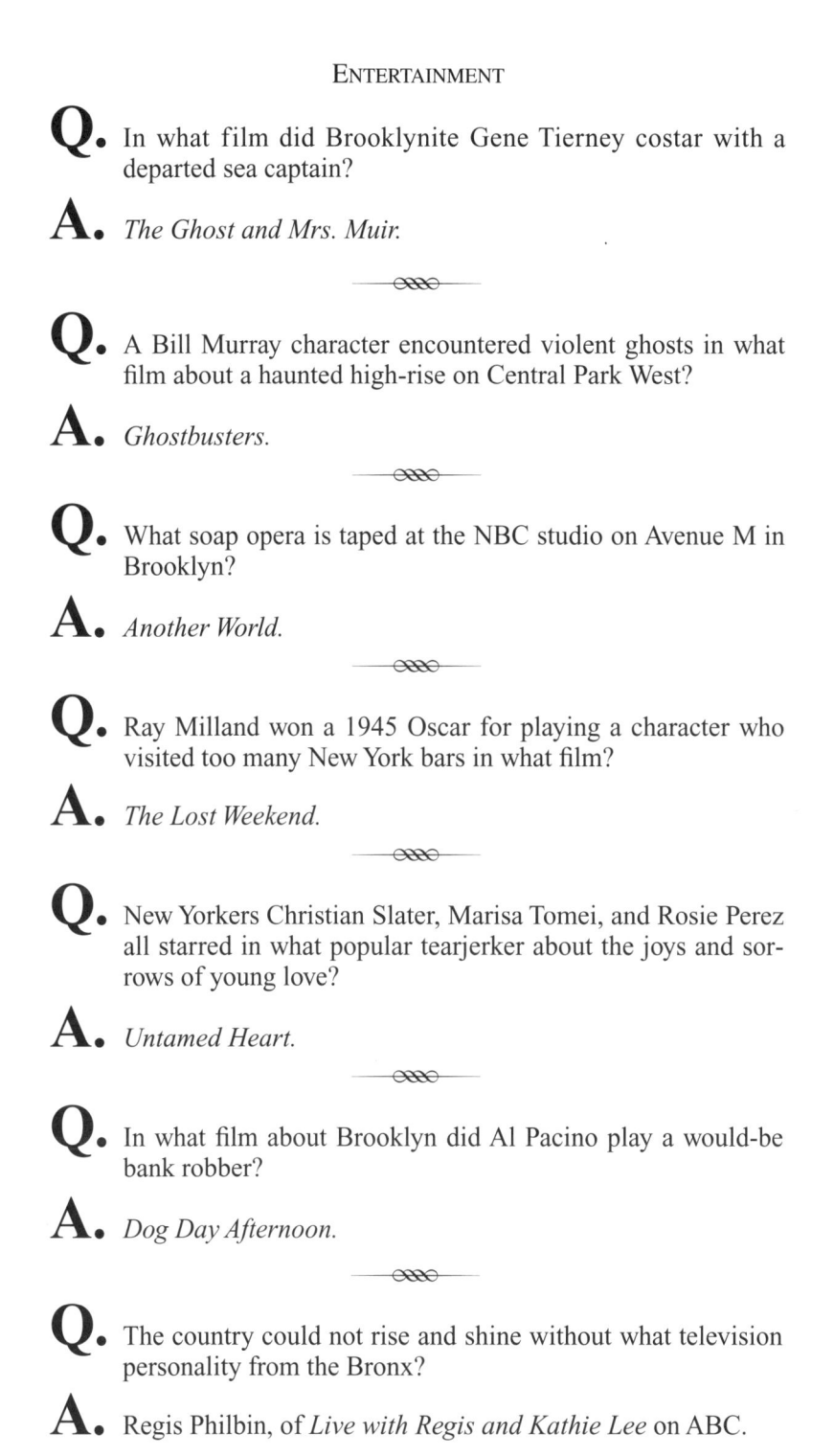

Q. In what film did Brooklynite Gene Tierney costar with a departed sea captain?

A. *The Ghost and Mrs. Muir.*

Q. A Bill Murray character encountered violent ghosts in what film about a haunted high-rise on Central Park West?

A. *Ghostbusters.*

Q. What soap opera is taped at the NBC studio on Avenue M in Brooklyn?

A. *Another World.*

Q. Ray Milland won a 1945 Oscar for playing a character who visited too many New York bars in what film?

A. *The Lost Weekend.*

Q. New Yorkers Christian Slater, Marisa Tomei, and Rosie Perez all starred in what popular tearjerker about the joys and sorrows of young love?

A. *Untamed Heart.*

Q. In what film about Brooklyn did Al Pacino play a would-be bank robber?

A. *Dog Day Afternoon.*

Q. The country could not rise and shine without what television personality from the Bronx?

A. Regis Philbin, of *Live with Regis and Kathie Lee* on ABC.

ENTERTAINMENT

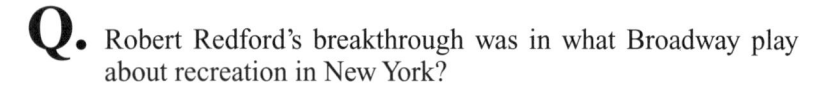

Q. Robert Redford's breakthrough was in what Broadway play about recreation in New York?

A. *Barefoot in the Park.*

Q. For what was Lindy's Restaurant in Times Square most famous?

A. Theatrical gossip and cheesecake.

Q. What was the big attraction at the Paradise nightclub in Times Square?

A. A chorus line of blue-eyed blondes.

Q. What former ragtime pianist and longtime Brooklynite wrote the most successful African-American show ever on Broadway?

A. Eubie Blake wrote *Shuffle Along.*

Q. During the early years of television, what comedian was a member of every family in the nation?

A. Milton "Uncle Milty" Berle.

Q. Who, on radio station WEAF in 1922, was the first sponsor of a commercial?

A. The Queensboro Realty Corporation.

Q. What two male singers from Brooklyn can pour out more feeling than all the other guys on the charts combined?

A. Barry Manilow and Neil Sedaka.

ENTERTAINMENT

Q. The artistry of guitarist Jimi Hendrix was discovered at what nightclub in Greenwich Village?

A. Café What.

Q. When *Fiddler on the Roof* opened on Broadway in 1966, what was Bette Midler's original role?

A. A member of the chorus.

Q. What was the first album of the grandfathers of punk rock, the New York Dolls?

A. *Personality Crisis* in 1973.

Q. Stevie Wonder recorded what song about the city in 1963?

A. "Manhattan at Six."

Q. Though he is from Albany in Georgia, Ray Charles included what song in his 1970 hit album *Genius Hits the Road*?

A. "New York's My Home."

Q. Radio station WOR has had three generations of talk-show hosts with what name?

A. John Gambling.

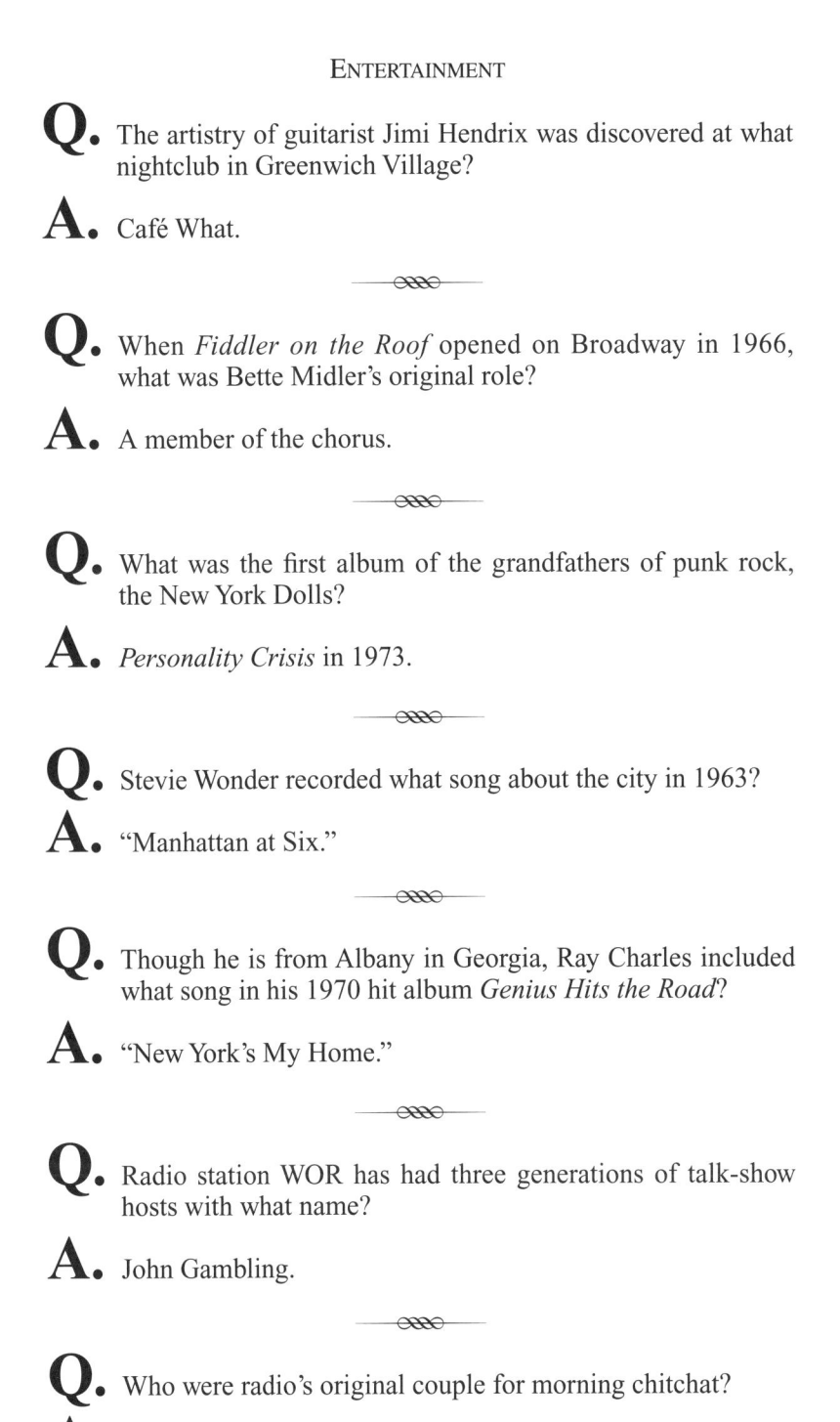

Q. Who were radio's original couple for morning chitchat?

A. WOR's Ed and Pegeen Fitzgerald.

ENTERTAINMENT

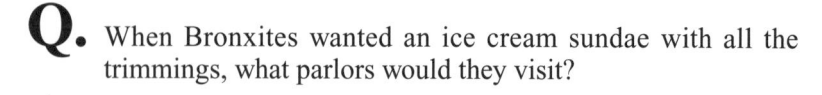

Q. When Bronxites wanted an ice cream sundae with all the trimmings, what parlors would they visit?

A. Krum's or Jahn's.

Q. To Bronxites, the world's most spectacular movie theater was and will always be what establishment on the Grand Concourse?

A. Loew's Paradise.

Q. What was the first station licensed for commercial television?

A. W2XBS on July 1941.

Q. In the 1990s, the Civil War was recreated with an Emmy Award–winning series by what documentarian for public television?

A. Ken Burns.

Q. At what comedy club did Billy Crystal get his start?

A. Pip's in Sheepshead Bay.

Q. What graduate of Forest Hills High in Queens became famous starring in a children's show?

A. Bob Keeshan, aka Captain Kangaroo.

Q. "Mrs. Robinson" and other songs in the award-winning film *The Graduate* were written by what graduates of Forest Hills High in Queens?

A. Paul Simon and Art Garfunkel.

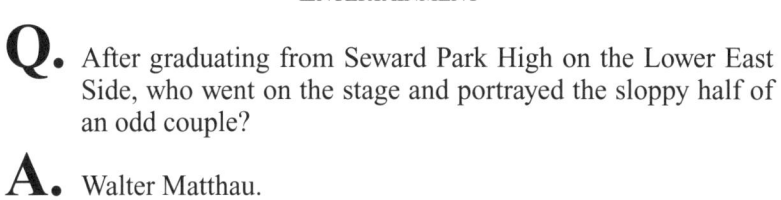

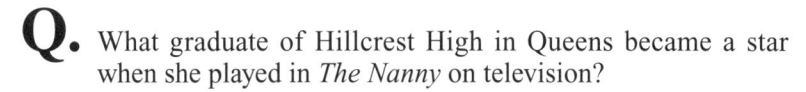

Entertainment

Q. After graduating from Seward Park High on the Lower East Side, who went on the stage and portrayed the sloppy half of an odd couple?

A. Walter Matthau.

Q. What graduate of Hillcrest High in Queens became a star when she played in *The Nanny* on television?

A. Fran Drescher.

Q. How did Mayors Fiorello LaGuardia and Rudolph Giuliani exercise the musical genius of their Italian ancestors?

A. LaGuardia conducted bands and orchestras. Giuliani did walk-ons at the Metropolitan Opera.

Q. At what Manhattan delis are you most likely to see a show biz celebrity eating a pastrami on rye?

A. The Stage (834 Seventh Avenue) and the Carnegie (854 Seventh Avenue).

Q. In 1951, who designed the eye that is the symbol of CBS television?

A. William Golden.

Q. Who was the first African-American performer to win a contract from a top movie studio?

A. Lena Horne.

Q. When and where can you go on a hayride in the city?

A. In September, at the Queens Country Fair.

ENTERTAINMENT

Q. A high school in Brooklyn is named for what award-winning television newscaster?

A. Edward R. Murrow.

Q. What was John Sebastian's big hit in 1976?

A. His theme song for the television show *Welcome Back, Kotter.*

Q. The soap opera *Another World,* taped in Brooklyn, was a stepping stone to stardom for what hunk from Oklahoma?

A. Brad Pitt.

Q. What comedian was born on a Lower East Side street that was named for an English prime minister?

A. George Burns of Pitt Street.

HISTORY

CHAPTER THREE

O! call back yesterday, bid time return.
—Shakespeare, *Richard II*

Q. When did the first Europeans arrive in New York?
A. In April 1524.

Q. Who were the first European visitors to what is now New York City?
A. Giovanni da Verrazano and his crew of forty-nine.

Q. What did Verrazano name the area he discovered?
A. Angoulême, a title of his patron, King Francis of France.

Q. Manhattan was the home of what Native-American tribe?
A. The Algonquins.

Q. The Algonquins were part of what organization of tribes that occupied not only Manhattan but also the Bronx?
A. The Wappinger Confederacy.

History

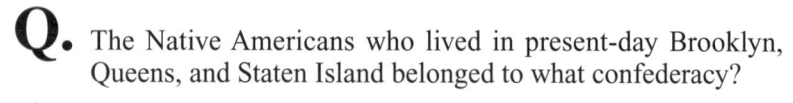

Q. The Native Americans who lived in present-day Brooklyn, Queens, and Staten Island belonged to what confederacy?

A. The Delaware.

Q. Ariel and Will Durant collaborated on what eleven-volume, prize-winning opus?

A. *The Story of Civilization.*

Q. In 1609, Dutch explorer Henry Hudson traveled the river now bearing his name in what ship?

A. The *New Moon.*

Q. New Amsterdam, as the Dutch named the city, was founded in what year?

A. 1615.

Q. What generous brother gave New Amsterdam to the duke of York on March 22, 1664?

A. King Charles II of England.

Q. For whom is New York named?

A. James Stuart, the duke of York.

Q. For whom is the borough of Queens named?

A. Catherine, wife of King Charles II.

History

Q. When was the borough of Brooklyn first settled?

A. 1634.

Q. Despite the legend about Peter Minuit, who really purchased Manhattan from the Native Americans in 1625?

A. Willem Verhulst, the director, or top honcho, of New Netherland.

Q. Before 1956, what was the name of Freedom Island, the site of the Statue of Liberty in New York Harbor?

A. Bedloe's Island.

Q. What is the official name of the Statue of Liberty?

A. Liberty Enlightening the World.

Q. When and by whom was the Statue of Liberty dedicated?

A. October 28, 1886, by President Grover Cleveland.

Q. From pedestal base to tip of its torch, how tall is the 225-ton Statue of Liberty?

A. Three hundred two feet and one inch.

Q. The Statue of Liberty's iron framework was built by the same engineer who worked on what other sizable structure?

A. The Eiffel Tower in Paris.

The Statue of Liberty, pride of New York City and symbol of freedom throughout the world. New York Convention and Visitors Bureau.

THE LADY IN THE HARBOR

One of the life's tasks of Édouard de Laboulaye, a French historian who wanted to rid the world of slavery, was the construction of a statue he called "Liberty Enlightening the World." In 1865, at a gathering of kindred spirits at his country house near Versailles, de Laboulaye enlisted the services of sculptor Frédéric Auguste Bartholdi. The project, a statue of a woman raising a torch in her right hand and holding a tablet with the date of the Declaration of Independence in her left hand, was soon on its way. They aimed for completion by 1876, the centennial of the Declaration of Independence. Bartholdi's wife, Jeanne, and his mother, Charlotte, were his models.

Intended to be a gift from the people of France to the people of America, the statue would inform oppressed people of the world that the liberty achieved in America was the birthright of all humanity. Raising the money for materials and workmen proved arduous, however, and Bartholdi declined a fee for his work. At its completion, the statue weighed 225 tons and stood 152 feet high. Its hand extended sixteen feet and its index finger eight feet. The structure needed a 150-foot high base to support it.

In May 1883, Charles Pomeroy Stone, a retired general in the Union army during the Civil War, paid several visits to Bedloe's Island in New York Harbor, the site chosen for the statue. He wanted to study its geologic structure to plan the engineering for a statue that would have to withstand winds of up to 145 miles an hour on the exposed ten-acre island.

By January 1884, long after General Stone had come, seen, and conquered the engineering problems, only fifteen feet of the pedestal had been built. The $150,000 raised by the statue's fundraisers in the United States was exhausted, and President Chester Alan Arthur's plea to Congress for an appropriation was killed in committee. Key congressmen did not believe all that much in liberty for all men, just as many did not believe in voting rights and equality for women.

Fortunately, the statue had made a favorable impression upon Joseph Pulitzer, an immigrant whose success story in America was a realization of the democratic vision expressed in Emma Lazarus's "The New Colossus," a contemporary poem about the Statue of Liberty. Pulitzer had arrived in 1864 from Hungary, which was ruled with an iron fist by the Hapsburg dynasty of Austria, and within twenty years he was owner and publisher of the New York *World*. On March 13, 1885, Pulitzer began an all-out campaign to raise the sum needed to complete the statue's pedestal. He started the ball rolling with a gift of one thousand dollars and a promise to print the names of all contributors in his newspaper.

The *World* received $101,091, mostly in small coins, from 120,000 Americans, and on June 17, 1885, General Stone boarded the French freighter *Isère* in New York Harbor and received the documents of transfer and the 139 crates that contained the statue. With a ceremony intended to reverberate around the world until all its inhabitants were free, the statue was dedicated by President Grover Cleveland on October 28, 1886.

History

Q. When did mail service begin in the city?
A. January 22, 1673.

Q. In 1653, what local hangout was converted into the first city hall?
A. The Stadt Huys tavern.

Q. The Boston Post Road, already busy in 1675, is now part of what national highway as it passes through the Bronx?
A. U.S. 1.

Q. How did the Peach War of 1643 start?
A. A Dutch official killed a Native-American woman picking peaches in his orchard.

Q. How far back do documents at the Hall of Records go?
A. 1653.

Q. When did the English take over the city from the Dutch?
A. September 8, 1664.

Q. On June 12, 1665, who became the first mayor of the city?
A. Thomas Willett.

History

Q. The principle of freedom of religion in the New World is due to the struggle of what early Quaker with the government?

A. John Bowne.

Q. In 1700, John Bowne's family was visited in Queens by what two founders of the Quaker religion?

A. William Penn and George Fox.

Q. The Dutch learned to prepare what perennially favorite snack food from Native Americans?

A. Popcorn.

Q. When did the city's first slave market open?

A. 1711.

Q. When was slavery abolished in New York?

A. 1827.

Q. In the country's first census, taken in 1790, what was the city's population?

A. 33,131.

Q. What was the first history book published in New York?

A. *A History of the Five Indian Nations* by Cadwallader Colden, in 1727.

History

Q. In what year did New York become the country's first city with one million people?

A. 1880.

Q. John Peter Zenger, whose trial in 1735 led to the establishment of freedom of the press, was the editor of what publication?

A. *New York Weekly Journal.*

Q. Where in Manhattan can you now hear the church bell that rang out in 1776 to proclaim the signing of the Declaration of Independence?

A. Middle Collegiate Church at Second Avenue and East Seventh Street.

Q. When did the U.S. Congress meet for its first regular session at Federal Hall in New York?

A. April 6, 1789.

Q. Why was the ceremony delayed when George Washington was sworn in as the first president on April 30, 1789?

A. A Bible had to be found before he could take the oath of office.

Q. In case you missed Washington's inaugural ball, where can you see the outfit he wore?

A. The Museum of the City of New York, 1220 Fifth Avenue.

Q. On July 11, 1804, what two local politicians engaged in the most famous duel in American history?

A. Former Treasury Secretary Alexander Hamilton and Vice President Aaron Burr. Hamilton was killed, and Burr became political poison and a social pariah.

History

Q. When was the first stock exchange started on Wall Street?

A. 1792, in a coffeehouse.

Q. Why did Aaron Burr challenge Alexander Hamilton to a duel in 1804?

A. Slander and insults were uttered from both sides; Hamilton had supported Jefferson over Burr for the presidency, and he frustrated Burr's bid to become governor of New York State.

Q. What were the actual last words of mortally wounded naval hero Capt. James Lawrence, who died in 1813 and is buried in Trinity Churchyard?

A. "Tell the men to fire faster and not to give up the ship; fight her till she sinks."

Q. What is Manhattan's oldest surviving church?

A. St. Paul's Chapel at Broadway and Fulton Street. The earliest section was built between 1764 and 1766.

Q. What future historian roller-skated to her wedding at city hall in 1913?

A. Ariel Durant.

Q. When did the Quakers, the Society of Friends, have their first meeting in New York?

A. 1687.

Q. Before the Civil War, the Friends' meetinghouse on East Twentieth Street was used for what secret purpose?

A. As part of the Underground Railroad to freedom for runaway slaves.

History

Q. The Roman Catholic Church has designated what saints as guardians for its congregants in the five boroughs?

A. St. Patrick for the Bronx, Manhattan, and Staten Island. The Blessed Virgin Mary, under the Title of the Immaculate Conception, for Brooklyn and Queens.

Q. New York City was the capital of the United States during what years?

A. From 1783 to 1789.

Q. What English organization sent over a mission to improve the city in 1880?

A. The Salvation Army.

Q. Willem Verhulst bought Manhattan for the equivalent in bolts of cloth and assorted trinkets of what sum?

A. Sixty guilders or twenty-four dollars.

Q. Early bureaucrat Willem Verhulst was banished from the city in 1626 for what crime?

A. Embezzling.

Q. What were the city's first exports?

A. Beaver and otter fur.

Q. What is the oldest surviving structure in the city and state?

A. The Pieter Claesen Wyckoff House in Brooklyn at 5900 Clarendon Road, which was built in 1652.

HISTORY

Q. From where do more famous Americans come than anywhere else in the country?

A. According to the New York Convention and Visitors Bureau, Brooklyn is the number-one birthplace of famous Americans, with one out of seven.

Q. It will never replace Solomon's Temple in Jerusalem, but what synagogue is the largest in the world?

A. Temple Emanu-El in Manhattan at Fifth Avenue and Sixty-fifth Street.

Q. What is the largest cathedral in the city and in the world?

A. St. John the Divine located at Amsterdam Avenue at West 112th Street in the Morningside Heights section of Manhattan.

Q. The nave of the Cathedral of St. John the Divine, the world's longest, is how many feet?

A. 601.

Q. What is the city's largest mosque?

A. Islamic Center of New York at Third Avenue and East Ninety-sixth Street.

Q. What is Voorlezer's House on Staten Island?

A. Built in 1695, it is the original "little red schoolhouse" in the country.

Q. What is one of the most famous ships ever built at the Brooklyn Naval Yard?

A. The battleship *Missouri,* on whose deck the Japanese signed the surrender ending World War II.

History

Q. Who lived in the Brooklyn community of Weeksville in the decades before the Civil War?

A. Freed slaves.

Q. Who was the first African-American woman elected to Congress?

A. Shirley Chisholm of Brooklyn elected in 1968.

Q. Against what form of government duress did New Yorkers riot for three days in 1863, resulting in nine hundred deaths and eight thousand injuries?

A. The military draft for the Civil War.

Q. In the 1850s, what world-renowned leftist was a foreign correspondent for the conservative *New York Tribune*?

A. Karl Marx.

Q. Henry George, author of *Progress and Poverty*, ran without success for what office in 1886?

A. Mayor of New York City.

Q. What Pulitzer Prize–winning author once ran for mayor of New York?

A. Norman Mailer, in 1969.

Q. From 1855 to 1892, about seven million immigrants passed through what station at the southern tip of Manhattan?

A. Castle Garden.

Ellis Island opened in 1892, and in the thirty years it served as the country's main immigration facility, five thousand people were processed daily. New York Convention and Visitors Bureau.

Q. In 1892, Castle Garden was replaced as an immigration center by what other facility?

A. Ellis Island.

Q. In 1857, what community of African Americans and poor European immigrants was destroyed so that Central Park could be built?

A. Seneca Village.

Q. What is the old Brooklyn legend of Barren Island?

A. According to the legend, Gibbs the pirate buried his treasure there.

History

Q. In 1690, what seafarer lived on Pearl Street near the East River and a fast escape?

A. Capt. William Kidd, the pirate who was hanged by the British in 1701.

Q. For what pious deed is Captain Kidd remembered?

A. He lent tackle and other ship equipment to build Trinity Church in 1696.

Q. Who was the first woman detective in the city and country?

A. Isabella Goodwin, in 1912.

Q. The Empire State Building has had how many visitors since it was completed in 1931?

A. 250,000,000.

Q. Who was the leading lady in the 1933 movie *King Kong*?

A. Fay Wray.

Q. What happened to the Empire State Building on July 28, 1945?

A. An army bomber crashed into it.

Q. What other landmark, now on Park Avenue, once occupied the site of the Empire State Building?

A. The Waldorf-Astoria Hotel.

History

Q. What Brooklynite was the first American cardinal?

A. Archbishop John McCloskey in 1875.

Q. What disaster took 147 lives in 1911 but resulted in better factory conditions for workers all over the city and country?

A. A fire at the Triangle Shirtwaist Company.

Q. Who was the longtime leader of the International Ladies Garment Workers Union of New York?

A. David Dubinsky.

Q. When did the *New York Times* and the *New York Daily News* begin publication?

A. September 18, 1851, and June 26, 1919, respectively.

Q. Who designed the statue of George Washington on the steps of the Federal Hall National Memorial on Wall Street?

A. John Quincy Adams Ward in 1883.

Q. In what historic church can you see a slave gallery?

A. St. Augustine's Episcopal on Henry Street on the Lower East Side, built in 1827.

Q. What devastation occurred on Wall Street on September 16, 1920?

A. A bomb explosion killed thirty and injured one hundred.

History

Q. What woman conducted a thriving blacksmith shop in early New Amsterdam?

A. Heilke Pieterse.

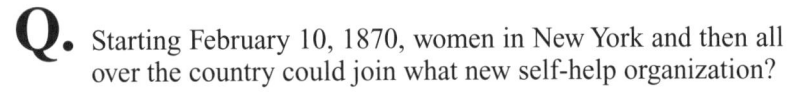

Q. Starting February 10, 1870, women in New York and then all over the country could join what new self-help organization?

A. The Young Women's Christian Association.

Q. When and where did A&P (the Great Atlantic and Pacific Tea Company) open its first grocery store in the country?

A. In 1859 on Vesey Street in Lower Manhattan.

Q. What Brooklynite was appointed to the U.S. Supreme Court in 1993?

A. Ruth Bader Ginsburg.

Q. On September 1, 1907, the city was the first in the country to conduct what sort of a judicial proceeding?

A. A session of night court.

Q. What royal troublemaker lived in exile in New York until he returned to his homeland and became emperor?

A. Napoleon III of France.

Q. What was the country's first African-American community newspaper?

A. *Freedom's Journal* published in 1827.

History

Q. Who, in 1811, designed city hall?

A. Joseph F. Mangin and John McComb Jr.

Q. When was the first horse-drawn streetcar in town?

A. 1832.

Q. When and what was Black Thursday?

A. October 24, 1929, the day the stock market crashed and started the Great Depression.

Q. What was the headline in *Variety,* the paper of show biz, when the New York Stock Exchange crashed on October 24, 1929?

A. "Wall Street Lays An Egg."

Q. Long popular in the Jewish community, when did bagels start catching on all over town?

A. About 1930.

Q. What is the distinction of the New York and Harlem Railroad Company, which began operations on April 14, 1832?

A. First street railway in the world.

Q. When did regular service start on the New York City subway system?

A. October 27, 1904.

History

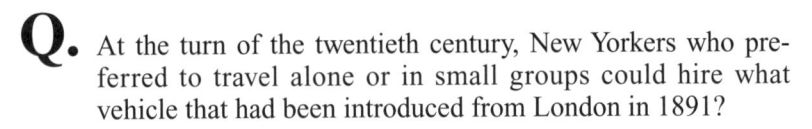

Q. At the turn of the twentieth century, New Yorkers who preferred to travel alone or in small groups could hire what vehicle that had been introduced from London in 1891?

A. A hansom cab.

Q. They are all gone now, but above what avenues did elevated trains once run in Manhattan?

A. Second, Third, Sixth, and Ninth.

Q. What was the last day of service on the Third Avenue elevated rail line?

A. January 12, 1955.

Q. Decades before McDonald's and Burger King, what fast-food restaurant in Coney Island was inventing and selling what all-American treat?

A. Nathan's, hot dogs.

Q. Before Coke and Pepsi, what drink did locals prefer with their hot dogs?

A. Root beer with a big head.

Q. Who not only fought for women's suffrage and the abolition of slavery but also wrote "The Battle Hymn of the Republic"?

A. Julia Ward Howe, in 1862.

Q. What Manhattan merchant began selling lace from his native Ireland and ended up with the world's biggest retail store in 1862?

A. Alexander Turney Stewart, owner of A. T. Stewart.

History

Q. It was the policy of the A. T. Stewart store to offer a 10 percent discount to what two professional groups and their families?

A. Clergymen and schoolteachers. The policy resulted in a proliferation of counterfeit "clergymen" and "teachers."

Q. What was the original name of Columbia University?

A. Kings College, founded in 1754.

Q. What was the theme of the World's Fair of 1939?

A. "The World of Tomorrow."

Q. Visitors will always remember what two gigantic symbols of the World's Fair of 1939?

A. The Trylon and the Perisphere.

Q. In reply to a young reader named Virginia, what journalist from the *New York Sun* affirmed that Santa Claus "lives and he lives forever"?

A. Frank Church, during the Christmas season of 1897.

Q. In what Brooklyn church was Confederate Gen. Thomas J. "Stonewall" Jackson baptized at age thirty?

A. St. John's Episcopal.

Q. What Confederate leader was once a vestryman at St. John's Episcopal Church in Brooklyn?

A. Gen. Robert E. Lee.

History

Q. Established in 1803, what is the oldest running newspaper in the country?

A. The *New York Post*.

Q. Who founded the *New York Post*?

A. Alexander Hamilton.

Q. After selling the *New York Post* in 1988, what international media magnate repurchased it in 1993?

A. Rupert Murdoch.

Q. In a great goof by the *Chicago Tribune,* what New Yorker was prematurely headlined as the thirty-third president in 1948?

A. Thomas E. Dewey. The headline was "DEWEY DEFEATS TRUMAN."

Q. Millions of Irish have come to New York City, but what New Yorker went to Ireland and became its prime minister in 1937?

A. Eamon de Valera.

Q. When did a bomb explode in a garage under the World Trade Center, killing six and injuring more than one thousand?

A. February 26, 1993.

Q. Where, opened in 1935, is First Houses, the prototype of public housing in America?

A. On Avenue A and East Third Street in Manhattan.

HISTORY

Q. On June 15, 1904, what excursion boat sank in local waters with more than one thousand casualties?

A. *General Slocum.*

Q. What New York politician was always asking, "How'm I doin'?"

A. Mayor Ed Koch.

Q. Mayor Ed Koch was doing okay until he was defeated in the 1989 primary by what other candidate?

A. David Dinkins.

Q. David Dinkins had the usual political virtues and a terrific game of tennis, but what attribute distinguished him from the city's 105 previous mayors?

A. He was the city's first African-American mayor.

Q. Three presidents were born in New York State, but which of the three was born in New York City?

A. Theodore Roosevelt.

Q. Barbara Pierce, born in the city June 8, 1925, is better known under what married name?

A. First Lady Barbara Bush.

Q. When Theodore Roosevelt organized his Rough Riders to fight in Cuba, at what upscale clothing shop did he buy his uniform?

A. Brooks Brothers.

History

Q. Established in 1818 and long on Madison Avenue, Brooks Brothers sells more of what garment than anything else?

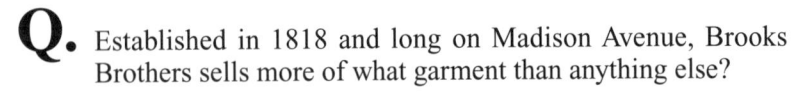

A. Oxford shirts with button-down collars.

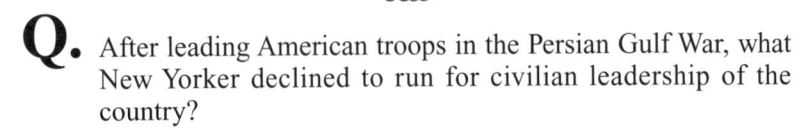

Q. After leading American troops in the Persian Gulf War, what New Yorker declined to run for civilian leadership of the country?

A. Gen. Colin Powell.

Q. From 1932 to 1984, Norman Vincent Peale officiated at what church on Fifth Avenue?

A. The Marble Collegiate Church, a Reformed Church in America, originally the Collegiate Reformed Dutch Church.

Q. Norman Vincent Peale distilled his learning and experience into what perennial best-seller?

A. *The Power of Positive Thinking,* published in 1952.

Q. In the mid-1800s, who headed Tammany Hall, the group that took crooked politics away from aristocrats and gave it to the common people "where it belonged"?

A. William Marcy "Boss" Tweed.

Q. In 1897, what organization was formed to keep municipal government honest and efficient?

A. Citizens Union.

Q. Women still could not vote in 1916, but what organization was formed that year to lobby city government?

A. The Women's City Club.

History

Q. When was the first police force established in New York?

A. 1658.

Q. Since the police are "New York's Finest," what do sanitation workers call themselves?

A. "New York's Strongest."

Q. On an average day, how many tons of garbage does the Sanitation Department pick up and haul off to the Fresh Kill landfill on Staten Island?

A. Fourteen thousand.

Q. When was the city's fire department established?

A. 1659.

Q. What is the nickname of Alphonse D'Amato, a local boy who became a U.S. senator and countrywide power broker in 1981?

A. Senator Pothole.

Q. The interior of Grant's Tomb, located on Riverside Drive in Manhattan, was inspired by the final resting place of what other military leader?

A. Emperor Napoleon of France.

Q. Where was the world's first church for congregants with impaired speech and hearing?

A. St. Ann's in Washington Heights.

History

Q. What was the first day of electric power for homes and businesses?

A. September 4, 1882.

Q. Who was the first New Yorker to free his slaves?

A. Charles Doughty in 1799.

Q. Patrons of what saloon, established in 1854, may invite you out to the alley if you dispute that it is the oldest of its kind in town?

A. McSorley's Old Ale House.

Q. When did McSorley's Old Ale House first admit women on its manly premises, and when was a woman's bathroom installed?

A. In 1970 and 1987 respectively. The slogan had been "Good Ale, Raw Onions, and No Ladies."

Q. What is the name of the mayor's official residence?

A. Gracie Mansion. It is located in Carl Schurz Park at East End Avenue at East Eighty-eighth Street.

Q. Who was the first mayor to live in Gracie Mansion?

A. Fiorello H. LaGuardia, in 1942.

Q. What, established in 1893, is the oldest organization of women artists and writers in the country?

A. Pen and Brush.

History

Q. At what unique location is New York's sea, air, and space museum?

A. Aboard the aircraft carrier USS *Intrepid* in the Hudson River.

Q. If your ancestors were poor immigrants in New York, where can you see their lifestyle replicated?

A. The Lower East Side Tenement Museum at 90 Orchard Street in Manhattan.

Q. What was the merchandise of Joseph Brewster, who in 1832 built Old Merchant's House, which still has all its original furniture?

A. Millinery.

Q. What New York resident returned to Russia and was a top Soviet leader until he was exiled to and then assassinated in Mexico?

A. Leon Trotsky.

Q. How did Russian immigrant Leon Trotsky earn a living while he lived in New York and plotted a revolution in his homeland?

A. As a movie extra.

Q. What New York resident returned to France and became its premier in 1906?

A. Georges Clemenceau.

Q. Founded in the city in 1973 was what civil rights group for homosexuals?

A. The National Gay and Lesbian Task Force.

History

Q. On June 27, 1969, a police raid at what Greenwich Village bar led to three days of riots and a gay rights movement that spread all over the world?

A. The Stonewall Inn.

Q. What hot dog and deli maker in the Bronx claims to enjoy a special relationship with a Higher Power?

A. Hebrew National.

Q. In 1776, the year of freedom, what group of local workers was the first in the nation to strike for more freedom from harsh employers?

A. The Journeymen Printers.

Q. What local workers settled a 114-day strike on April 1, 1963?

A. Newspapermen.

Q. Because it is the alma mater of Pat Robertson, what school can claim to be the spiritual birthplace of the Christian Coalition?

A. The New York Theological Seminary.

Q. Since 1892, hundreds of ambassadors and ten presidents have and bought their cutaways and tuxedos at what Manhattan establishment?

A. A. T. Harris Formalwear.

Q. What New Yorker, born in 1774, became the first American-born saint of the Catholic Church?

A. Elizabeth Ann Seton, founder of the Sisters of Charity and of many schools and colleges, was canonized in 1975.

History

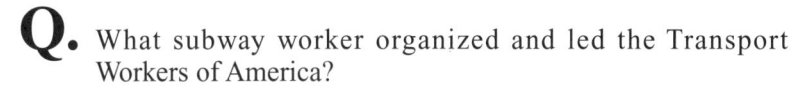

Q. What subway worker organized and led the Transport Workers of America?

A. Mike Quill.

Q. Whose funeral, stretching for eleven blocks, was the largest ever held in the city?

A. Rudolph Valentino, the Latin lover of the silent screen, who died on August 23, 1926.

Q. Who, in 1831, was the city's first bank robber?

A. Edward Smith, who stole $245,000 and was sentenced to three years in the slammer.

Q. What bakery still bakes the kind of bread whose preparation is described in the Old Testament?

A. The Streit Matzoth Company, at 150 Rivington Street on the Lower East Side.

Q. How were New Yorkers finally convinced that the Brooklyn Bridge, formally opened on May 24, 1883, was safe for pedestrians?

A. Circus impresario P. T. Barnum led twenty-one of his elephants across it.

Q. What and when was the first professional theater in New York City?

A. The Theater on Nassau Street in 1750. Its first offering was Shakespeare's *Richard III*.

Q. Who organized and became president of the National Maritime Union from 1937 until 1973?

A. Big Joe Curran.

Brooklyn Bridge, pictured here around 1900, was the longest suspension bridge in the world when it was completed in 1883. Underwood Photo Archives, S.F.

THE EIGHTH WONDER OF THE WORLD

Connecting Brooklyn and Lower Manhattan over the East River, the Brooklyn Bridge was the world's first steel-wire suspension bridge. At its completion in 1883, it was also the world's longest suspension bridge, with a main span of 1,595 feet, a length of 7,580 feet, and granite towers that soared 272 feet above mean high water. The bridge almost was not built, because Manhattan businessmen feared competition from Brooklyn, and would offer neither money nor support for its construction.

After years of political and commercial intrigue by its prime advocate, State Senator Henry C. Murphy of Brooklyn, the bridge was hardly begun in 1869 when its designer and head of operations, John Augustus Roebling, crushed a foot and died of tetanus a few days later. He was quickly replaced by his son and protégé Washington Augustus, who had been an engineer for the Union army during the Civil War.

Foundations for the bridge were built in underwater chambers sunk to forty-four feet on the Brooklyn side and seventy-eight feet on the Manhattan side. Two pairs of cables supported steel suspenders that upheld a roadway platform eighty-six feet wide. Each cable, composed of 5,296 galvanized steel wires, could sustain a load of 12,000 tons. The total length of wire in the four cables was 14,357 miles—half the circumference of the planet.

By 1872, the younger Roebling was among the more than one hundred men who were permanently crippled with decompression sickness, and until the completion of the bridge he could view it only through field glasses from his bedroom window. On-site operations were taken over by his wife Emily, who had mastered math and engineering.

The original estimate for building the bridge was $4 million, but it cost $18 million and the lives of twenty of its builders.

Shaded by her parasol, Emily Roebling was the first person to ride across the bridge early in 1883. On May 24, 1883, with flags fluttering and brass bands blaring, the bridge was formally opened by President Chester Alan Arthur, New York Gov. Grover Cleveland, Mayor Franklin Edson of New York City, and Mayor Seth Low of Brooklyn. Afterward, the dignitaries marched to the Roeblings' home in gratitude for their spectacular contribution to the beauty and progress of the two cities and the whole country.

As for average Brooklynites and New Yorkers, they were intimidated for a while by the length and height of the bridge, and by its strange wires and cables. Their fears were put to rest when circus impresario Phineas T. Barnum performed another one of his publicity stunts and led twenty-one of his well-fed elephants across the bridge to prove its soundness.

History

Q. Around 1860, when guests checked in at respectable hotels such as the Astor House, with what house rule did they have to comply?

A. Leave their guns in the cloakroom.

Q. What is the motto of the *New York Times*?

A. "All the News That's Fit to Print."

Q. What does the *Daily News* claim to be?

A. "New York's Hometown Newspaper."

Q. What has been the most popular Jewish newspaper in the city and country since 1897?

A. The *Jewish Forward*.

Q. Early readers of the *Jewish Forward* turned at once to what essential feature?

A. "A Bintel Breev," offering advice to the lovelorn and perplexed.

Q. A half century after his death in 1947, for what is Mayor LaGuardia most remembered?

A. On July 1, 1945, he read the Sunday funnies on the radio during a newspaper strike.

Q. During a newspaper strike, what Sunday comic did Mayor LaGuardia, strong on law and order, read on the radio with special feeling?

A. "Dick Tracy."

History

Q. Joe's Saloon on East Fourteenth Street in Manhattan was the inspiration for what popular poem of yesteryear?

A. "The Face on the Barroom Floor," written by Hugh A. D'Arcy in 1887.

Q. What New Yorker organized the American Federation of Labor?

A. Samuel Gompers.

Q. What, started in 1871, was the first rapid transit system in New York City?

A. The Ninth Avenue Elevated train.

Q. When was the original Pennsylvania Station built?

A. 1910.

Q. Back in the days when a free lunch was still available in bars, what was usually the pièce de résistance?

A. Meatballs or, depending on size, meat marbles.

Q. To avail yourself of a free lunch at a bar, what was the minimum purchase of drink?

A. A mug of beer.

Q. Even after failing to become president in 1928, what four-time New York State governor from the Lower East Side continued to call himself "The Happy Warrior"?

A. Alfred E. Smith.

History

Q. What article of attire was Governor Al Smith reputed to wear even in bed?

A. A derby.

Q. What famous political and military leaders lie in the graveyard of St. Mark's Church in-the-Bowery in the East Village?

A. Governor Peter Stuyvesant and Commodore Matthew C. Perry.

Q. What local schoolboy grew up and became a leader of teachers across the country?

A. Albert Shanker, president of the American Federation of Teachers.

Q. In 1866, who founded the American Society for the Prevention of Cruelty to Animals in New York City?

A. Henry Bergh.

Q. What was the world's first hotel with an elevator?

A. The Fifth Avenue, in 1859.

Q. Who, in 1884, organized the country's first newspaper syndicate?

A. Samuel Sidney McClure.

Q. Early in the twentieth century, what Jewish civil rights leader became a founder and then president of the NAACP?

A. Joel Spingarn.

History

Q. As famous for her wide-brimmed hats as for her salty speeches was what congresswoman from the Upper West Side of Manhattan?

A. Battling Bella Abzug, who served from 1971 to 1976.

Q. What was the campaign slogan of political activist Bella Abzug when she ran for Congress?

A. "A woman's place is in the house—the House of Representatives!"

Q. Decades before he became president, John F. Kennedy attended what grade school in the Bronx?

A. Riverdale Country School.

Q. President John Tyler was married in what church on Fifth Avenue?

A. The Church of the Ascension, in 1844.

Q. When explorer David Livingstone was lost in Africa in 1871, what newspaper dispatched Henry Stanley to find him?

A. The *New York Herald*.

Q. How did Henry Stanley greet David Livingstone when he tracked him down in Africa?

A. "Dr. Livingstone, I presume."

Q. What happened in a Bronx cemetery, St. Raymond's, in April 1932?

A. Bruno Hauptmann received a $50,000 ransom for the promised return of the Lindbergh baby.

History

Q. At what cemetery were the sexes once segregated?

A. The Moravian Cemetery on Staten Island.

Q. In the 1930s, why was financier Hetty Green called the Witch of Wall Street?

A. Because she always dressed in black and could outfox male financiers and stockbrokers.

Q. During the male-dominated 1860s, what was the vocation of Hell-Cat Maggie?

A. She led a gang of Bowery hoods.

Q. What municipal hospital on First Avenue between East Twenty-sixth and East Thirtieth Streets is the oldest general hospital in North America?

A. Bellevue, established in 1734.

Q. All through the 1930s and 1940s, what fast-food chain had a daily breakfast special of orange drink, a donut, and coffee for a dime?

A. Nedick's.

Q. Where, during the 1930s and 1940s, could you get a hot dog and a root beer for a dime?

A. Ruby's, a small chain in Manhattan.

Q. What was a popular Bronx newspaper that was absorbed by the *New York Post*?

A. The *Home News*.

History

Q. What is the *New York Social Register*?

A. A listing of the socially elite by reason of birth and respectability.

Q. To what store, first on Ladies' Mile, and now in Herald Square, could Gay Nineties entertainer Lillian Russell have hustled for a new bustle?

A. R. H. Macy's, established in 1858.

Q. Gimbel's department store, the longtime rival of R. H. Macy in Herald Square, had what slogan?

A. "Nobody, but nobody undersells Gimbel's."

Q. What was once a unique free service at Gimbel's department store?

A. If you bought artificial flowers, a Japanese expert would arrange them in your vase or bowl.

Q. Established in 1879 and lasting almost a century, what was the name of the department at Best & Company that catered to the clothing and furniture needs of kids under age six?

A. The Lilliputian Bazaar.

Q. When and where did Samuel Lord, the founding father of the Lord & Taylor department store on Fifth Avenue, open his first dry goods shop?

A. 1850, in the Queens village of Newtown.

Q. In 1909, what organization was formed in New York to protect the morals of moviegoers across the country?

A. The National Board of Censorship.

The United Nations complex is situated along the East River on an eighteen-acre site that was donated by the Rockefeller family in 1952. New York Convention and Visitors Bureau.

Q. What New Yorker paid $1 million for a new church in his neighborhood so that he could get to it in time for a seat on Sunday?

A. Railroad tycoon Thomas Fortune Ryan.

Q. Thanks to the generosity of what family did the United Nations acquire the land to establish its headquarters in New York?

A. The Rockefellers in 1952.

Q. Who was assassinated on February 21, 1965, at the Audubon Ballroom in Washington Heights?

A. Civil rights activist Malcolm X.

Q. What Brooklyn gangsters of the 1930s had a more businesslike name than is possessed by the average mob?

A. Murder, Inc.

History

Q. Ever since 1799, the Flatbush Dutch Reformed Church in Brooklyn has performed what function?

A. Tolled the death of presidents.

Q. Who is the most famous dropout of Erasmus Hall High School, the public school that emanated from Erasmus Hall Academy in Brooklyn?

A. Chess champion Bobby Fischer.

Q. To fight discrimination, what society did the city's Irish establish in 1836?

A. The Ancient Order of Hibernians.

Q. Sure, and when was the first St. Patrick's Day Parade up Fifth Avenue?

A. 1852.

Q. In May and June, what great parades are held on Fifth Avenue?

A. Parades honoring Martin Luther King Jr. and Puerto Rican Day respectively.

Q. Attracting huge crowds in Little Italy every mid-September is what annual event?

A. The Feast of San Gennaro.

Q. When was the biggest ticker-tape parade on lower Broadway?

A. March 1, 1962, when an estimated 3,474 tons were dropped upon astronaut John Glenn.

History

Q. When did the Dutch permit Jews to settle in New Amsterdam?

A. 1654.

Q. Established in 1654, what is the oldest Jewish congregation in New York City and the country?

A. Shearith Israel. Its synagogue is now located at 99 Central Park West.

Q. A poem by Emma Lazarus (1849–1887), one of Shearith Israel's congregants, is inscribed on what symbol of freedom?

A. The Statue of Liberty.

Q. How many women marched in the city for the right to vote on October 27, 1917?

A. About twenty thousand.

Q. When did New York State adopt a constitutional amendment that gave women the right to vote?

A. November 6, 1917.

Q. What historical event occurred at the Stephen Wise Free Synagogue on August 1, 1972?

A. The installation of Sally Jane Preisand, the first woman rabbi in the country.

Q. What does the Martyrs' Monument in Brooklyn's Fort Greene Park commemorate?

A. The eleven thousand patriots who died nearby on British prison ships during the Revolutionary War.

History

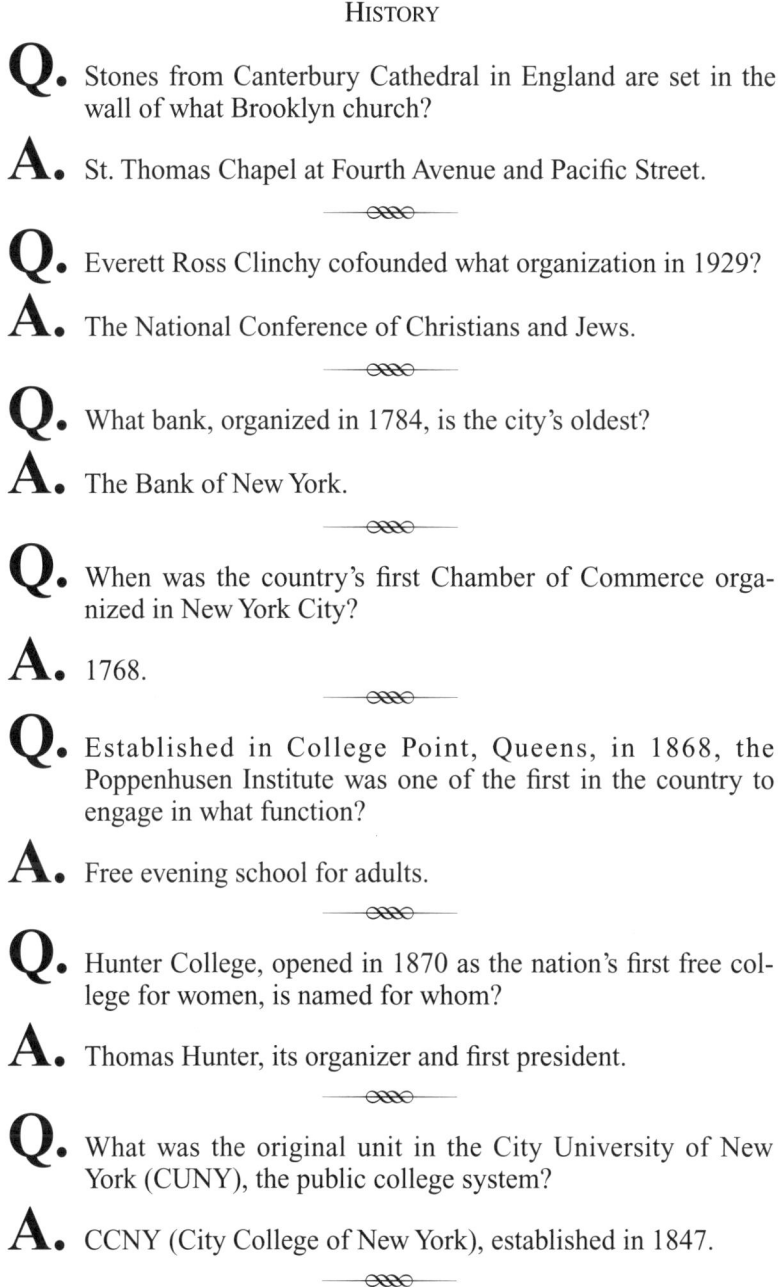

Q. Stones from Canterbury Cathedral in England are set in the wall of what Brooklyn church?

A. St. Thomas Chapel at Fourth Avenue and Pacific Street.

Q. Everett Ross Clinchy cofounded what organization in 1929?

A. The National Conference of Christians and Jews.

Q. What bank, organized in 1784, is the city's oldest?

A. The Bank of New York.

Q. When was the country's first Chamber of Commerce organized in New York City?

A. 1768.

Q. Established in College Point, Queens, in 1868, the Poppenhusen Institute was one of the first in the country to engage in what function?

A. Free evening school for adults.

Q. Hunter College, opened in 1870 as the nation's first free college for women, is named for whom?

A. Thomas Hunter, its organizer and first president.

Q. What was the original unit in the City University of New York (CUNY), the public college system?

A. CCNY (City College of New York), established in 1847.

Q. What municipal college bears the name of an activist for African-American rights?

A. Medgar Evers.

History

Q. What municipal college is named for a Jewish philanthropist, financier, and presidential adviser?

A. Bernard M. Baruch, who coined the phrase "Cold War."

Q. When was the city's first automobile accident?

A. May 30, 1896.

Q. How many models were displayed at the country's first automobile show at the old Madison Square Garden in 1900?

A. Fifty-one.

Q. In what year did New Yorkers first have to buy license plates for their cars, and how much did the license plates cost?

A. License plates became compulsory in 1901, and they cost one dollar.

Q. What church group based in the Bronx broadcast the country's first radio sermon in 1921?

A. The Radio Church of America.

Q. Where, early in the nineteenth century, did a French nobleman lock up his daughter and her lower-class lover in a dungeon?

A. Bodine Castle in Queens.

Q. Opened in 1885 for an upscale clientele, the Osborne Apartments on West Fifty-seventh Street had what unusual amenity?

A. A croquet lawn on the roof.

HISTORY

Q. In addition to the very few private shelters, at what public facility could the city's homeless find refuge during most of the nineteenth century?

A. Police stations.

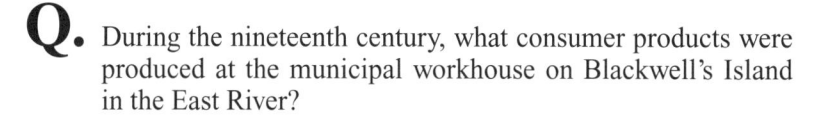

Q. During the nineteenth century, what consumer products were produced at the municipal workhouse on Blackwell's Island in the East River?

A. Cigars for men, hoopskirt forms for women.

Q. The old Pennsylvania Station, which began operations in 1910, was built to resemble what wonder of the ancient world?

A. The baths of Emperor Caracalla in Rome.

Q. When and where did the country's first Turkish bath open?

A. 1863, in Brooklyn.

Q. In 1933, at the height of the Great Depression, human rights activist Dorothy Day started what national movement?

A. The Catholic Worker.

Q. During the Great Depression, when did police attack thirty-five thousand unemployed New Yorkers who were demonstrating for government aid?

A. March 6, 1930.

Q. In the 1930s, socialites who cared for their daughters would want them to have their coming-out party at what "in" establishment on Fifth Avenue?

A. The Hotel Pierre.

History

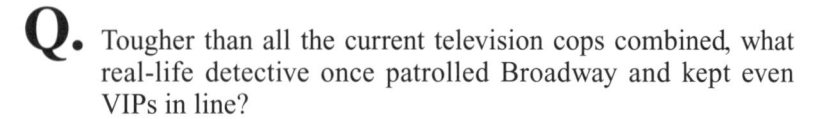

Q. Tougher than all the current television cops combined, what real-life detective once patrolled Broadway and kept even VIPs in line?

A. Johnny Broderick, "the Broadway Cop."

Q. George Bush's opponent for vice president in 1984 was what congresswoman from Queens?

A. Geraldine Ferraro.

Q. New York City has yet to have a woman mayor, but it has contributed what senator to Congress?

A. Barbara Boxer of California.

Q. What happened in New York on the night of November 9, 1965?

A. Lasting at least fourteen hours in most areas, the biggest power failure in the city's history.

Q. When did trolley cars complete their final route in Brooklyn?

A. October 31, 1956.

Q. When disreputable politician Aaron Burr married wealthy widow Eliza Brown Jumel in 1833, why did respectable New Yorkers regard them as birds of a feather?

A. Unaccompanied by her husband, Eliza had gone to France for a long vacation and returned pregnant.

Q. Aaron and Eliza Burr lived in domestic disharmony for how long before their divorce?

A. One year.

ARTS & LITERATURE
C H A P T E R   F O U R

To have great poets, there must be great audiences too.
—Walt Whitman

Q. Who wrote that no one should come to New York to live unless he is willing to be lucky?

A. E. B. White.

Q. What is the title of E. B. White's authoritative book about the city?

A. *Here Is New York.*

Q. Who, in 1524, was the city's first writer?

A. Giovanni da Verrazano wrote a diary and letters about his discovery of the city.

Q. Now a world center of publishing, New York saw its first press set up in 1693 by what printer?

A. William Bradford.

Q. When William Bradford published the city's first newspaper in 1725, what did he call it?

A. The *Gazette*.

— 117 —

ARTS & LITERATURE

Q. Who wrote a humorous history of the city in 1809?

A. Washington Irving wrote *Knickerbocker's History of New York*.

Q. The Library of Congress is now in Washington, D.C., but what library served that purpose while the federal government was in the city for a few years starting in 1789?

A. New York Society Library.

Q. Barnes & Noble opened its first bookstore at what Manhattan address in 1917?

A. 31 West Fifteenth Street.

Q. What Maine poet, a three-time winner of the Pulitzer Prize, once supported himself as a laborer on the New York subway?

A. Edwin Arlington Robinson.

Q. In what year did Columbia University Press release the first edition of *The Columbia Encyclopedia*?

A. 1935.

Q. What is the size of the Great Rose Window at the Cathedral of St. John the Divine in Manhattan?

A. Forty feet in diameter, with more than ten thousand pieces of stained glass.

Q. What event of interest to book lovers is held on Fifth Avenue in late September?

A. New York Is Book Country Fair.

Arts & Literature

Q. In what hotel did dramatist Tennessee Williams live and die?

A. The Elysee on East Fifty-fourth Street.

Q. When did the Metropolitan Museum of Art open to the public?

A. February 20, 1872.

Q. The Metropolitan Museum of Art paid $2.3 million, the highest price ever at the time, to obtain what Rembrandt painting in 1961?

A. *Aristotle Contemplating the Bust of Homer.*

Q. During the 1950s, the golden age of comic books, what was the message of a frequent sign in candy stores all over town?

A. "THIS IS NOT A LIBRARY!"

Q. How did Walt Whitman describe his relationship to the city?

A. "Walt Whitman am I, a Kosmos, of mighty Manhattan the son."

Q. What three Brooklyn newspapers did Walt Whitman edit?

A. The *Daily Eagle,* the *Brooklyn Freeman,* and the *Brooklyn Times.*

Q. What president wrote a history of New York City?

A. Theodore Roosevelt.

Q. What Brooklynite was a longtime publisher of a business magazine that proclaimed itself to be a capitalist tool?

A. Malcolm Forbes of *Forbes* magazine.

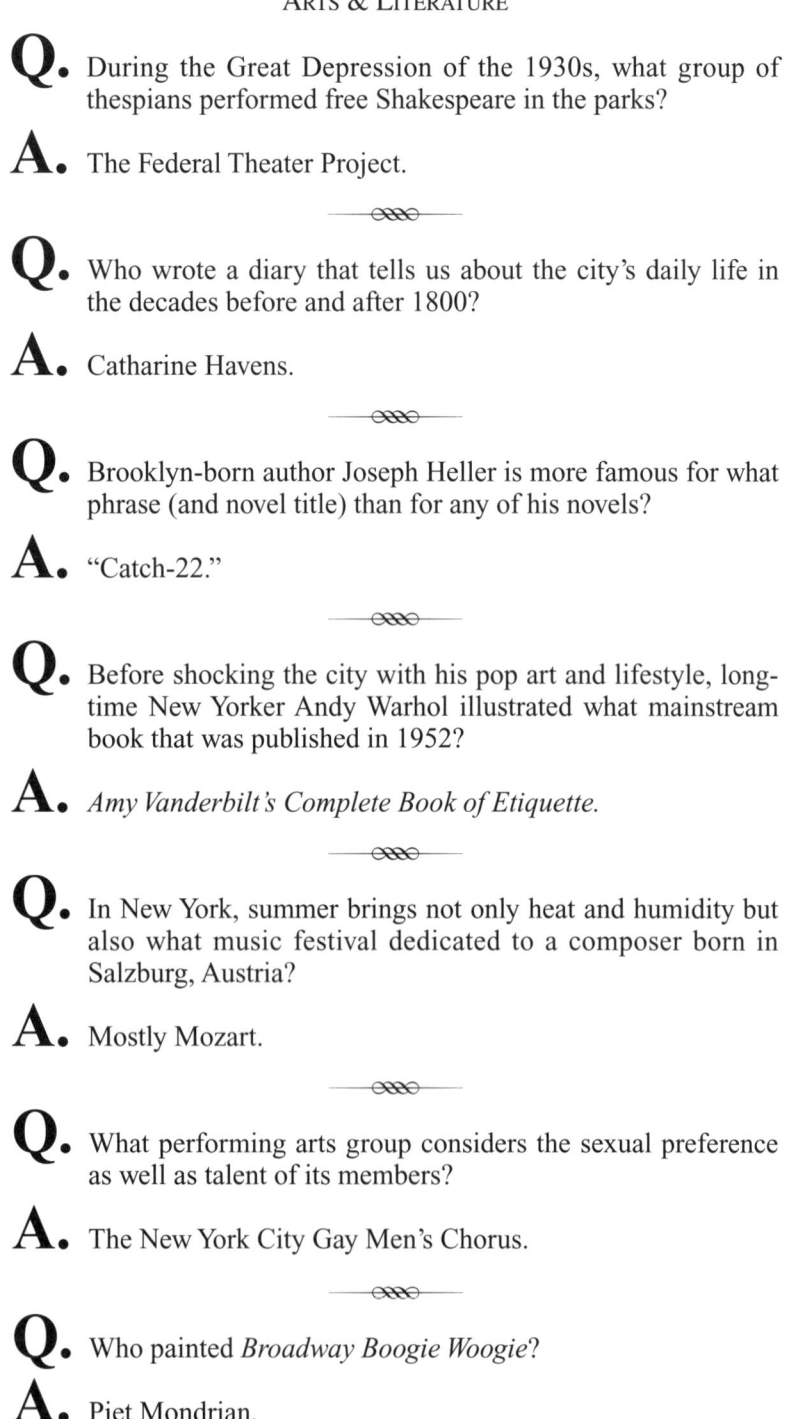

Arts & Literature

Q. During the Great Depression of the 1930s, what group of thespians performed free Shakespeare in the parks?

A. The Federal Theater Project.

Q. Who wrote a diary that tells us about the city's daily life in the decades before and after 1800?

A. Catharine Havens.

Q. Brooklyn-born author Joseph Heller is more famous for what phrase (and novel title) than for any of his novels?

A. "Catch-22."

Q. Before shocking the city with his pop art and lifestyle, long-time New Yorker Andy Warhol illustrated what mainstream book that was published in 1952?

A. *Amy Vanderbilt's Complete Book of Etiquette.*

Q. In New York, summer brings not only heat and humidity but also what music festival dedicated to a composer born in Salzburg, Austria?

A. Mostly Mozart.

Q. What performing arts group considers the sexual preference as well as talent of its members?

A. The New York City Gay Men's Chorus.

Q. Who painted *Broadway Boogie Woogie*?

A. Piet Mondrian.

Arts & Literature

Q. Van Gogh fans can see *Starry Night* at what museum?

A. The Museum of Modern Art.

Q. Which of Herman Melville's tales takes place entirely in New York?

A. *Bartleby the Scrivener.*

Q. Authorship of "Rip Van Winkle" and "The Legend of Sleepy Hollow" made what writer the Stephen King of 1820?

A. Washington Irving.

Q. The mother of what great English novelist wrote a book about New Yorkers in 1832?

A. Anthony Trollope.

Q. After a long tour of inspection, what was the title of Frances Trollope's sharp commentary in 1832 about the city and country?

A. *Domestic Manners of the Americans.*

Q. Who was the city's master of Gothic architecture during the nineteenth century?

A. Bertram Grosvenor Goodhue.

Q. What is regarded as the masterpiece of architect Bertram Grosvenor Goodhue and also the most beautiful church in the city?

A. St. Thomas Church on Fifth Avenue and West Fifty-third Street.

Arts & Literature

Q. What ruthless robber baron of the late 1800s tried to make amends by posthumously opening his mansion and art collection to the public?

A. Henry Clay Frick, the Frick Collection, 1 East Seventieth Street.

Q. When it comes to songs, what has remained New York's golden oldie since about 1900?

A. "The Sidewalks of New York," by James W. Blake and Charles Lawlor.

Q. What local novelist wrote a bestseller titled *East Side, West Side*?

A. Marcia Davenport.

Q. In what language did I. B. Singer write the novels that won him the Nobel Prize in 1978?

A. Yiddish.

Q. What Yiddish writer, buried in Queens, wrote the stories that became the award-winning play and film *Fiddler on the Roof*?

A. Sholem Aleichem.

Q. What author of *Love Story* may have found his own first love in Brooklyn?

A. Eric Segal.

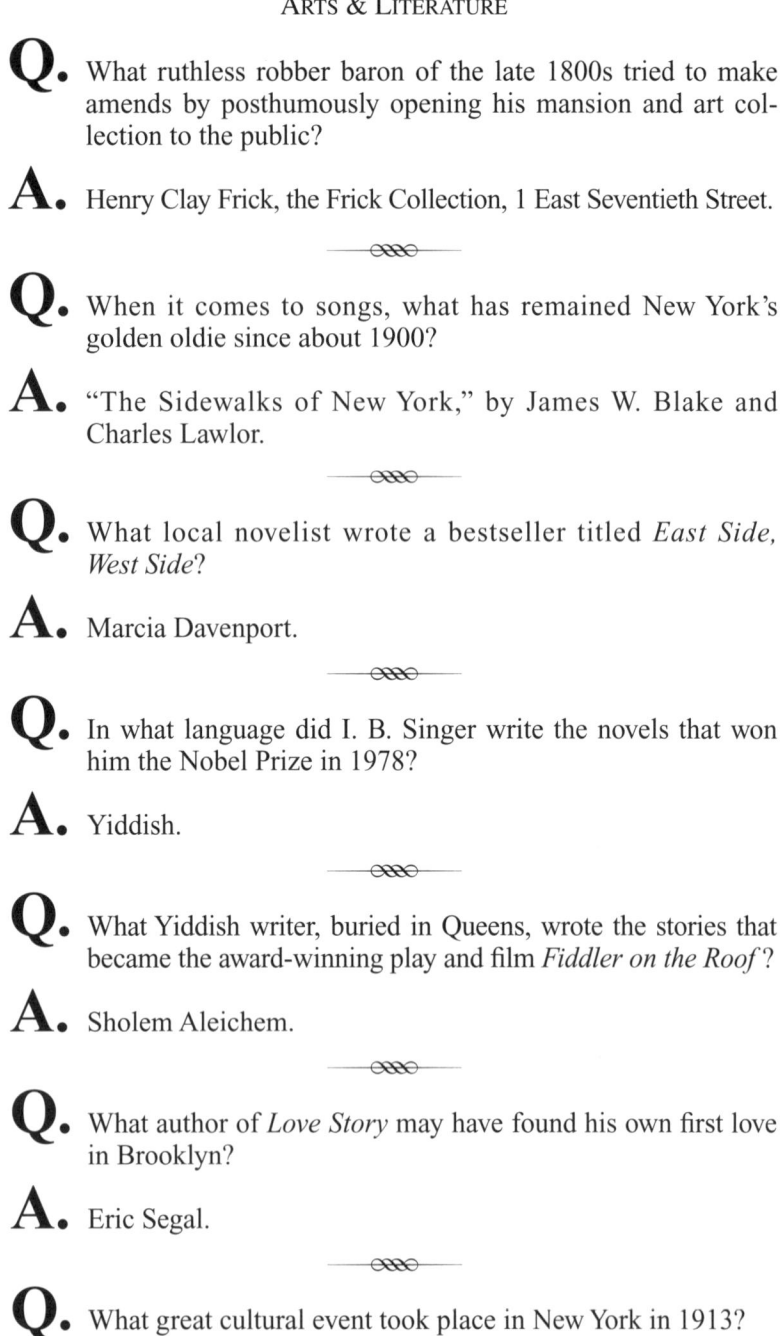

Q. What great cultural event took place in New York in 1913?

A. The Armory Show, which introduced the French impressionists to the city and country.

Arts & Literature

Q. The Empire State Building was designed by what firm?

A. Shreve, Lamb, and Harmon.

Q. John La Farge's greatest mural, *The Ascension,* can be seen in what church on Fifth Avenue?

A. The Church of the Ascension at West Tenth Street.

Q. The city's skyline inspired what composition by John Alden Carpenter?

A. *Skyscrapers, A Ballet of American Life.*

Q. After graduating from Yale, what New Yorker founded the *National Review* in 1955?

A. William F. Buckley Jr.

Q. Performed in the city in 1796 was what first American opera?

A. *The Archers, or the Mountaineers of Switzerland.*

Q. Who was the first African American to sing an important role at the Metropolitan Opera?

A. Marian Anderson. On January 7, 1955, she sang Ulrica in Verdi's *A Masked Ball.*

Q. What was the Met's first opera composed by a woman?

A. *Der Wald* by Ethel Mary Smith in 1903.

Majestic skyscrapers dominate the famed New York City skyline. New York Convention and Visitors Bureau.

Arts & Literature

Q. When did James Levine make his conducting debut at the Metropolitan Opera?

A. 1971.

Q. Who, in 1943, became the first artistic director of the New York City Opera?

A. Lazlo Halasz.

Q. Beverly Sills directed the New York City Opera during what years?

A. From 1979 to 1989.

Q. George Balanchine and Lincoln Kirstein formed what ballet company in 1948?

A. The New York City Ballet.

Q. For what children's ballet did Queens dancer Edward Villella win an Emmy?

A. *Harlequin.*

Q. What firm of architects is responsible for more New York City landmarks than any five others combined?

A. McKim, Mead and White.

Q. Clarence Day wrote what book about his New York childhood that became a bestseller and then a successful play and film?

A. *Life with Father.*

Arts & Literature

Q. The country's most prestigious awards for excellence in journalism and the arts, started in 1917, are in honor of what local publisher?

A. Joseph Pulitzer.

Q. Baseball and Civil War authority Doris Kearns Goodwin won the 1995 Pulitzer Prize in history for what book about Franklin and Eleanor Roosevelt?

A. *No Ordinary Time.*

Q. "September Song" was immortalized by Walter Huston in what 1938 play about old New York?

A. *Knickerbocker Holiday,* with book by Maxwell Anderson and music by Kurt Weill.

Q. What theater group performs the works of only a single playwright and composer?

A. The New York Gilbert and Sullivan Players.

Q. In 1931, Lower East Sider Fannie Hurst wrote what book that is now regarded as the mother of all tearjerkers?

A. *Back Street.*

Q. What Czech composer lived in Stuyvesant Square in Manhattan, and composed in 1893 a symphony that adapted the spirituals of African-American slaves?

A. Antonin Dvorak, Symphony No. 5 in E Minor (From the New World).

Q. The son of what great English novelist is buried in Trinity Church Cemetery in Washington Heights?

A. Charles Dickens. His son's given names were Alfred Tennyson.

Arts & Literature

Q. If you cannot wait to see your child's painting in a museum, where can she join a workshop and display her masterpiece that very day?

A. The Children's Museum of Manhattan at 212 West Eighty-third Street.

Q. Elvis Presley became a national phenomenon after gyrating on the prime-time television show of what local columnist?

A. Ed Sullivan.

Q. What is America's oldest center for the performing arts?

A. The Brooklyn Academy of Music, open since 1859.

Q. In 1850, when a New York lithographer and printer named Nathaniel Currier took in a partner, what was the name of their new enterprise?

A. Currier & Ives.

Q. In the 1870s, whose cartoons in *Harper's* magazine contributed to the decline of Boss Tweed and Tammany Hall?

A. Thomas Nast.

Q. In the 1920s, whose cartoons in the *Masses* failed to bring down Wall Street and capitalism?

A. Art Young.

Q. In whose home library, now open to the public, should a visitor not be surprised to see the first printed edition of Dante's *Divine Comedy* and a manuscript of *Paradise Lost* by John Milton?

A. J. P. Morgan at 29 East Thirty-sixth Street.

Arts & Literature

Q. Among the centers of attraction at the Black Fashion Museum, at 157 West 126th Street, is a dress designed by what civil rights leader?

A. Rosa Parks.

Q. In 1935, an exhibition of whose paintings put the Museum of Modern Art on the map?

A. Vincent van Gogh.

Q. In *American Notes,* Charles Dickens wrote about what New Yorkers who were as vicious as Bill Sikes in *Oliver Twist*?

A. Gangsters in the Five Points district.

Q. English novelist Anthony Trollope had what to say about New Yorkers in 1861?

A. "Every man worships the dollar, and is down before his shrine from morning till night." He also wrote that the women had never been taught good manners or behavior.

Q. Did Anthony Trollope admire anything about the city?

A. The free public schools were better than the ones in London.

Q. What building on Sixth Avenue (the Avenue of the Americas) was inspired by a royal castle in Bavaria?

A. The Jefferson Market Library at West Tenth Street.

Q. Historians James Harvey Robinson and Charles A. Beard founded what Greenwich Village school in 1919?

A. The New School for Social Research.

Arts & Literature

Q. In what Greenwich Village movie theater did patrons get a free demitasse with their double feature?

A. The Art Theater.

Q. Where could Lower East Siders enjoy free chamber music during the Great Depression?

A. The Educational Alliance on East Broadway and Jefferson Street.

Q. In the early days of radio and for decades afterward, who announced the Saturday broadcasts of the Metropolitan Opera?

A. Milton Cross, from 1931 to 1975.

Q. The Rolling Stones and Isaac Stern, the Beatles and Beverly Sills—they all performed at what concert hall on West Fifty-seventh Street?

A. Carnegie Hall.

Q. In 1891, who conducted one of the first concerts at Carnegie Hall?

A. Peter Ilich Tchaikovsky.

Q. During the 1940s and 1950s, what street musician played outside Carnegie Hall for coins and bills?

A. Professor Giuseppe Ravita, aka Little Paganini.

Q. What painter specialized in abstractions of the Brooklyn Bridge?

A. Joseph Stella.

The first bridge to link Manhattan and Brooklyn, the Brooklyn Bridge has inspired poets and artists for more than one hundred years. New York Convention and Visitors Bureau.

Q. If your taste in art runs to twentieth-century Americans, what museum with ten thousand works by them should you visit?

A. The Whitney Museum of American Art on Madison Avenue at East Seventy-fifth Street.

Q. The Whitney Museum is now on swanky Madison Avenue, but what was its more modest address when it was founded in 1931?

A. 8–12 West Eighth Street.

Q. Who was Thomas Wolfe's overworked editor at Scribner's?

A. Maxwell Perkins.

Q. Thomas Wolfe wrote what story about Brooklyn?

A. "Only the Dead Know Brooklyn."

Arts & Literature

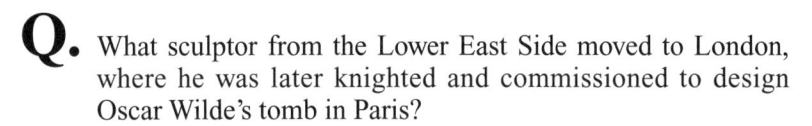

Q. What sculptor from the Lower East Side moved to London, where he was later knighted and commissioned to design Oscar Wilde's tomb in Paris?

A. Sir Jacob Epstein.

Q. What was the distinction of Dean Dixon when he conducted the New York Philharmonic in 1944?

A. He was the first African American to lead a major orchestra in the country.

Q. Painters as different as Jackson Pollock and Norman Rockwell have studied at what art school?

A. The Art Students League of New York.

Q. What novelist fathered *The Godfather* and therefore deserves a lot of respect?

A. Mario Puzo.

Q. How did Lorenzo Da Ponte, Mozart's librettist, earn a living in New York?

A. As a distiller and a professor of Italian at Columbia University.

Q. On PBS's *Masterpiece Theater*, what two New Yorkers have been able to hold their own with Charles Dickens and Jane Austen?

A. Edith Wharton and Henry James.

Q. Which of Henry James's stories is also an opera?

A. *The Turn of the Screw* by Benjamin Britten.

Arts & Literature

Q. In *The Fire Next Time,* published in 1963, what African American wrote that racial violence would continue for a long time in the land?

A. James Baldwin.

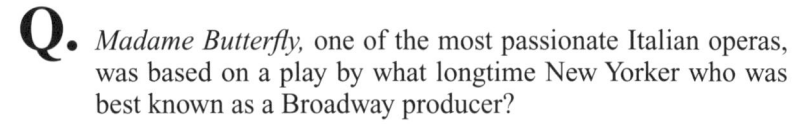

Q. *Madame Butterfly,* one of the most passionate Italian operas, was based on a play by what longtime New Yorker who was best known as a Broadway producer?

A. David Belasco.

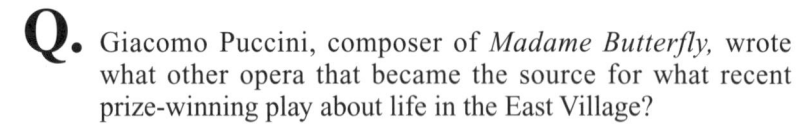

Q. Giacomo Puccini, composer of *Madame Butterfly,* wrote what other opera that became the source for what recent prize-winning play about life in the East Village?

A. *La Bohème* and *Rent.*

Q. What nightclub was named for jazz great Charlie Parker?

A. Birdland.

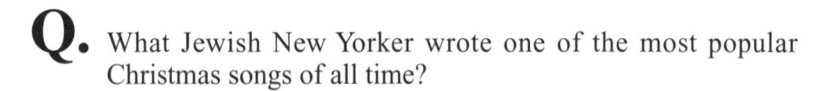

Q. What Jewish New Yorker wrote one of the most popular Christmas songs of all time?

A. Irving Berlin wrote "White Christmas."

Q. At what Chinatown bar did Irving Berlin begin his musical career as a singing waiter?

A. The Chatham Club.

Q. Muckraker Jacob Riis wrote what book that led to more humane housing and working conditions for the poor of the city and the country?

A. *How the Other Half Lives.*

Arts & Literature

Q. In the 1930s and 1940s, what Bowery bar became a hangout for tourists?

A. Sammy's Bowery Follies.

Q. The original itinerary of St. Nicholas and his reindeer was conceived by what local poet and scholar of ancient Hebrew?

A. Clement Clarke Moore in "The Night Before Christmas."

Q. Where in town is the Temple of Dendur from ancient Egypt?

A. The Metropolitan Museum of Art.

Q. Where is New York's Museum Mile?

A. On Fifth Avenue between Seventy-ninth and 104th Streets.

Q. Leonard Bernstein, originally from Lowell, Massachusetts, wrote what two musicals about his adopted city?

A. *On the Town* and *West Side Story*.

Q. What poet from New York City published *Leaves of Grass*?

A. Walt Whitman. It was published in 1855.

Q. What can be found at the Cloisters in Manhattan's Fort Tryon Park?

A. The medieval art collection of the Metropolitan Museum of Art.

Arts & Literature

Q. In 1851, more than a century before *Jaws,* what New Yorker wrote about the pursuit of a homicidal sea creature?

A. Herman Melville wrote *Moby Dick.*

Q. Which of Herman Melville's tales takes place entirely in New York?

A. *Bartleby the Scrivener.*

Q. What was the first department store in the city to have a full-scale art gallery?

A. Lord & Taylor.

Q. For what kind of artistry is Lord & Taylor's department store (Fifth Avenue at West Thirty-ninth Street) famous at Christmas?

A. Its decorated windows.

Q. What three New Yorkers created the ballet *Rodeo*?

A. Composer Aaron Copland, choreographer Agnes de Mille, and dancer Michael Kidd.

Q. Jacqueline Kennedy Onassis worked for what New York publisher?

A. Doubleday.

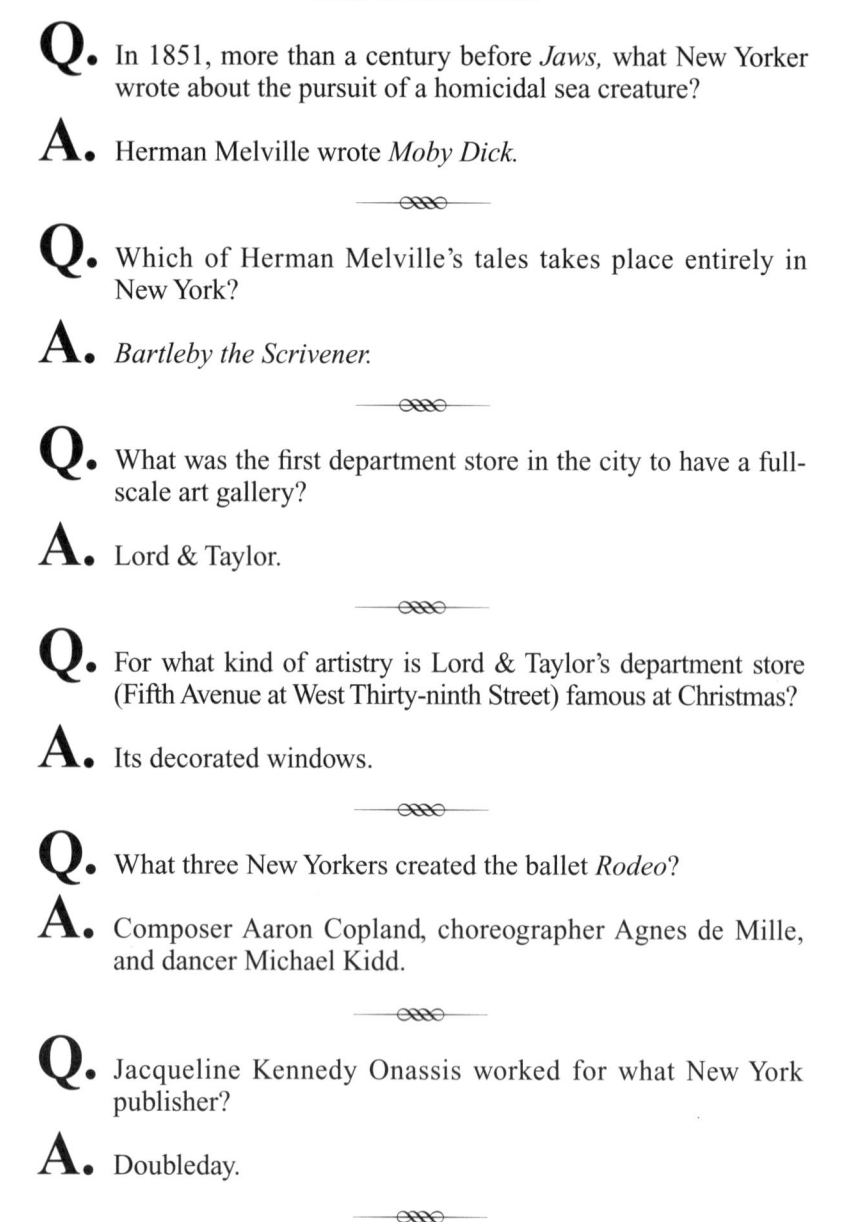

Q. Shortly after opening a studio in New York, Mathew B. Brady, famed later for his Civil War photos, published what series of portraits in 1850?

A. *Gallery of Illustrious Americans.*

Arts & Literature

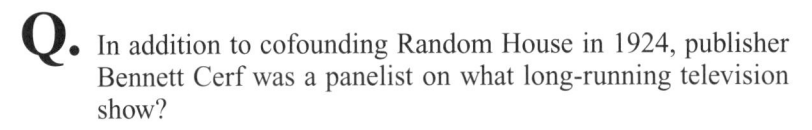

Q. In addition to cofounding Random House in 1924, publisher Bennett Cerf was a panelist on what long-running television show?

A. *What's My Line?*

Q. Ever since the late 1920s, Random House has published what line of classic books at a modest price?

A. The Modern Library.

Q. In 1939, Pocket Books introduced the first mass-market American paperbacks with what bestseller, and for how much?

A. *Lost Horizons.* It sold for a quarter.

Q. Who was the mascot and symbol of Pocket Books, headed by Robert de Graff?

A. Gertrude the kangaroo.

Q. On July 21, 1959, a New York federal court lifted the ban on what sexy book that would be considered quaint in a few years?

A. *Lady Chatterley's Lover* by D. H. Lawrence.

Q. What is the current name of the *Weekly Trade Journal*, founded in 1872 to report the news in book publishing?

A. *Publishers Weekly.*

Q. Published in 1867, the first of the more than one hundred inspirational novels by Horatio Alger bore what title?

A. *Ragged Dick: or Street Life in New York.*

ARTS & LITERATURE

Q. Sidney Kingsley wrote what play about New York street life in 1935?

A. *Dead End.*

Q. Where can television fans catch up with the installments of *The Honeymooners* and *Star Trek* that they once missed?

A. The Museum of Television and Radio at 25 West Fifty-second Street.

Q. In addition to tourists and tall buildings, you can also view gigantic statues of what two figures from Greek mythology in Rockefeller Center?

A. Prometheus and Atlas.

Q. At whose New York City bar gathered the greatest guzzlers in the history of the American theater?

A. Harry Hope's in *The Iceman Cometh* by Eugene O'Neill.

Q. *Death of a Salesman* was written by what Brooklynite?

A. Arthur Miller.

Q. Until his downsizing and death, what brand of automobile was preferred by Willy Loman, the traveling salesman in Arthur Miller's play?

A. Chevrolet.

Q. Daniel Day-Lewis starred in the film based on what book about the city's upper crust in the mid-1850s?

A. *The Age of Innocence.*

Arts & Literature

Q. Brooklynite Aaron Copland won a Pulitzer Prize for what tone poem about a season of the year?

A. *Appalachian Spring.*

Q. The music from what firm of piano makers in Queens can be heard around the world?

A. Steinway and Sons.

Q. Owners of frisky pets should keep them far away from the precious lamps and vases created by what New Yorker?

A. Louis Comfort Tiffany.

Q. What was the collective name for Greenwich Village painters who specialized in everyday life?

A. The Ashcan School.

Q. Long before tenor Luciano Pavarotti, what musician from Queens was using a handkerchief onstage?

A. Louis "Satchmo" Armstrong.

Q. Who sang "The Lord's Prayer" at Louis Armstrong's funeral?

A. Peggy Lee.

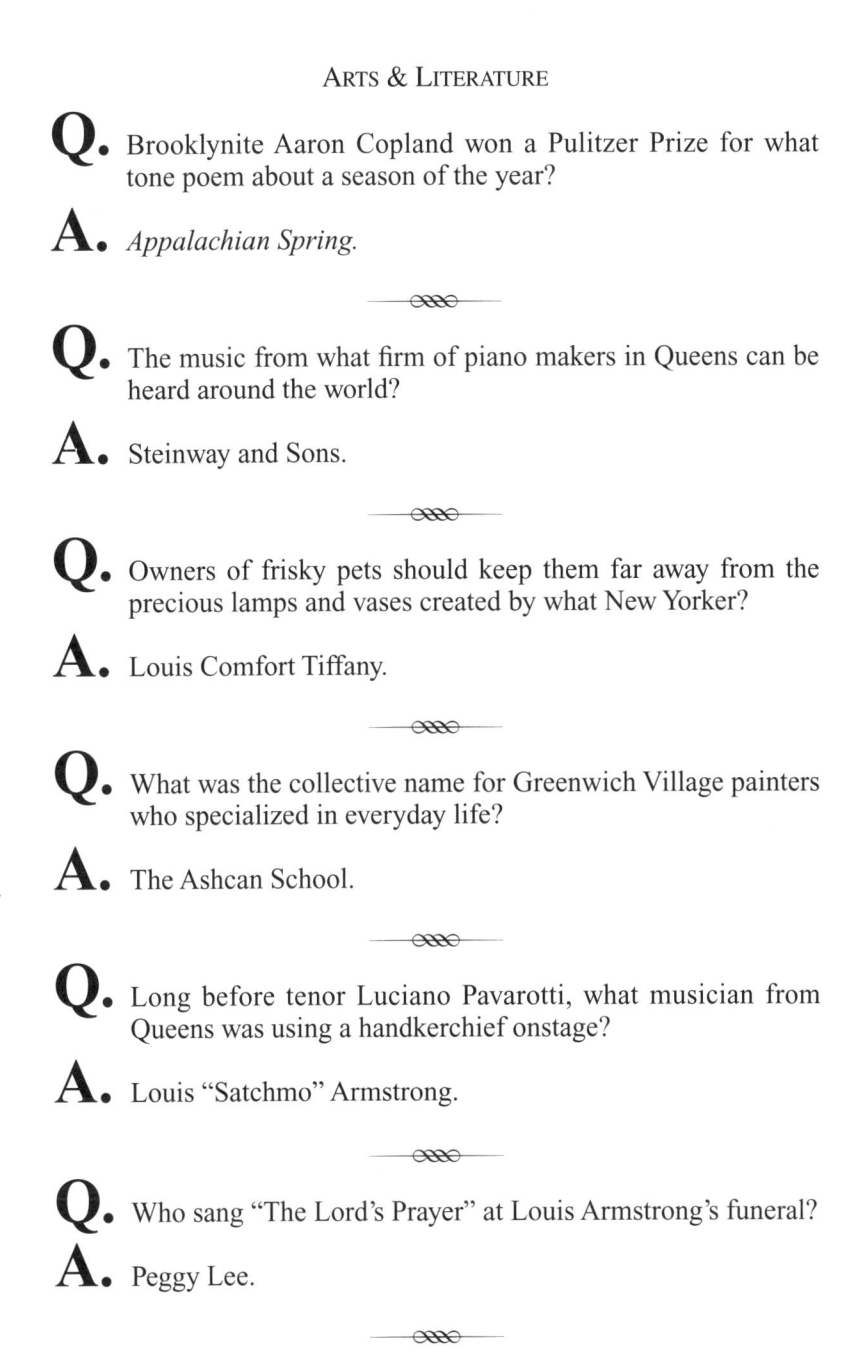

Q. First appearing in the *New York World* in 1896, what cartoon character soon became as popular as Charlie Brown is today?

A. The Yellow Kid of Hogan's Alley.

Arts & Literature

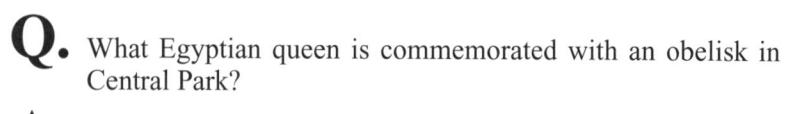

Q. What Egyptian queen is commemorated with an obelisk in Central Park?

A. Cleopatra.

Q. What *New York Times* columnist was once a speechwriter for President Nixon?

A. William Safire.

Q. Thanks to what local literary expert was the Book of the Month Club able to choose its monthly books for so many decades?

A. Clifton Fadiman.

Q. Harold Ross of Aspen, Colorado, established what magazine that is synonymous with big-town sophistication?

A. The *New Yorker.*

Q. What was the original motto of the *New Yorker*?

A. "Not for the Old Lady in Dubuque."

Q. What are the names of the concrete lions that guard the forty million items in the New York Public Library on Fifth Avenue at Forty-second Street?

A. Patience and Fortitude.

Q. Where did Truman Capote hold his "party of the century" on November 28, 1966?

A. The Plaza Hotel.

Arts & Literature

Q. What was mandatory attire at Truman Capote's lavish party at the Plaza Hotel?

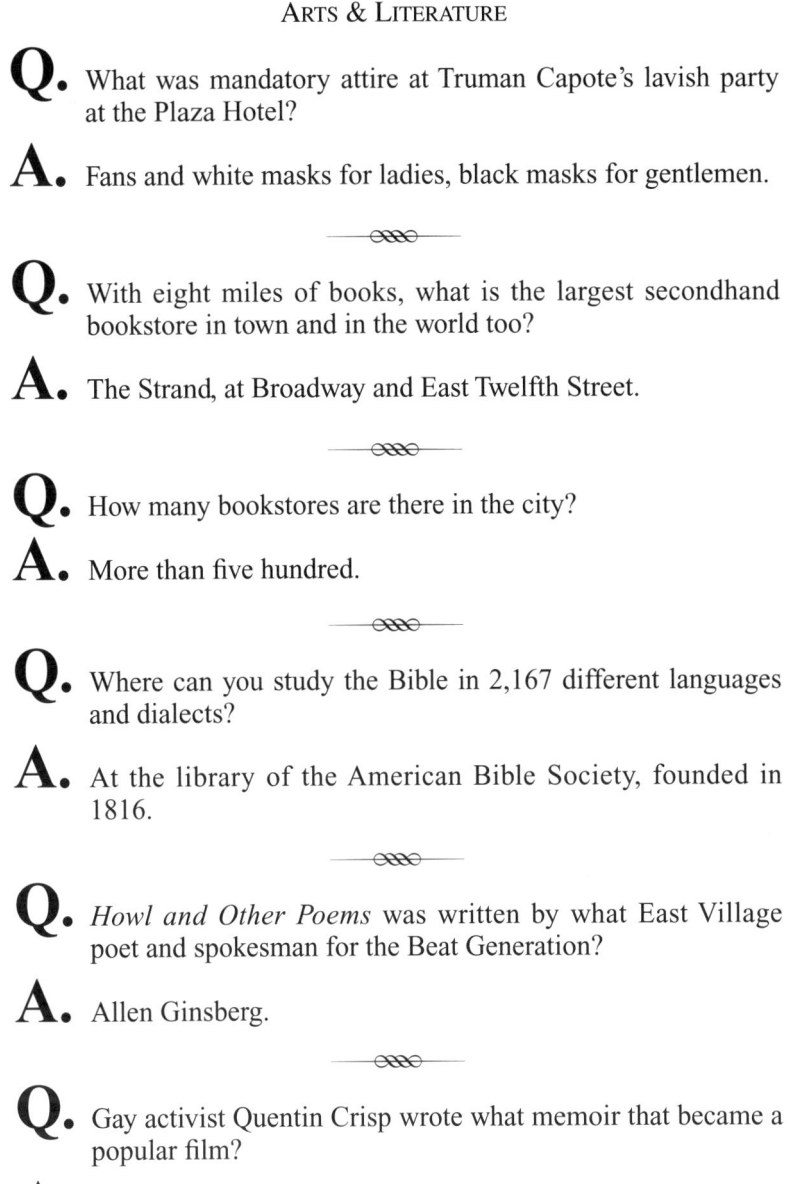

A. Fans and white masks for ladies, black masks for gentlemen.

Q. With eight miles of books, what is the largest secondhand bookstore in town and in the world too?

A. The Strand, at Broadway and East Twelfth Street.

Q. How many bookstores are there in the city?

A. More than five hundred.

Q. Where can you study the Bible in 2,167 different languages and dialects?

A. At the library of the American Bible Society, founded in 1816.

Q. *Howl and Other Poems* was written by what East Village poet and spokesman for the Beat Generation?

A. Allen Ginsberg.

Q. Gay activist Quentin Crisp wrote what memoir that became a popular film?

A. *The Naked Civil Servant.*

Q. Where can visitors buy a hometown newspaper in Manhattan?

A. Hotalings News Agency at 142 West Forty-second Street.

Arts & Literature

Q. In 1906, who was the first president to win a Nobel Peace Prize, and for what service did he win it?

A. Theodore Roosevelt for negotiating a peace treaty between Russia and Japan in 1906.

Q. How do patrons who do not know Italian or German understand what is going on at the Metropolitan Opera and the New York City Opera?

A. Above-stage projection of the libretto in English.

Q. Maya Lin, designer of the Vietnam Veterans Memorial in Washington, D.C., designed also the interior of what local institution?

A. The Museum for African Art at 593 Broadway.

Q. How much will you have to pay for the best seat at the Metropolitan Opera in Lincoln Center?

A. $250.

Q. In the 1830s, what earlier organization was offering serious music to the public?

A. New York Sacred Music Society.

Q. In 1883, what was the first opera performed at the original Met on Broadway and Thirty-ninth Street?

A. *Faust* by Charles Gounod.

Q. In what opera did Italian tenor Enrico Caruso make his New York debut on November 23, 1903?

A. *Rigoletto* by Verdi.

Arts & Literature

Q. In what opera did Irish tenor John McCormack debut at the Manhattan Opera House on November 10, 1909?

A. Verdi's *La Traviata*.

Q. With what company did President Reagan's son Ron dance for a few years?

A. Joffrey Ballet.

Q. How many museums and galleries can you expect to encounter in New York?

A. More than 550.

Q. Should you decide to stay in New York and get a college degree, you will have a choice of how many institutions of higher learning?

A. Ninety-four.

Q. If a raven at the Bronx Zoo ever wants to rest on a mantel instead of a tree, at whose nearby cottage will it not be welcome?

A. Edgar Allan Poe's in Poe Park, 2640 Grand Concourse, the Bronx.

Q. Frederic Dannay and Manfred B. Lee, two Brooklyn writers, created what single detective?

A. Ellery Queen.

Q. Who wrote *The Brooklyn Murders*?

A. G. D. H. Cole.

Arts & Literature

Q. The toys of your great-grandmother may be worthy of exhibit in what museum?

A. American Craft Museum at 40 West Fifty-third Street.

Q. It does not include a full-size pyramid, but where is the largest collection of Egyptian art in the Western Hemisphere?

A. The Brooklyn Museum at Eastern Parkway and Washington Avenue.

Q. If you are a fan of Tibetan and Algerian films, where is the place to see them?

A. The Anthology Film Archives on Second Avenue at East Second Street.

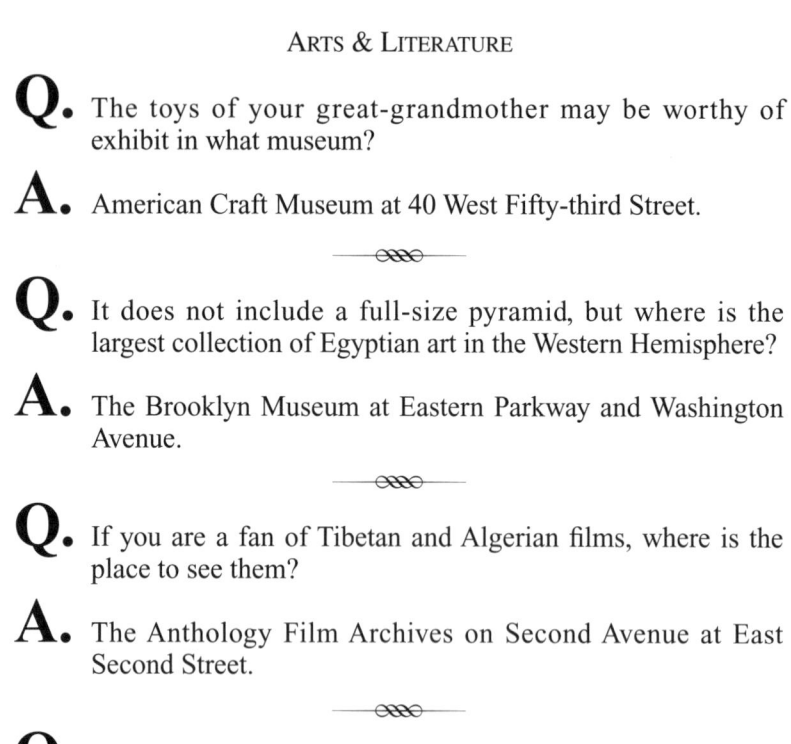

Q. What Welsh poet died in St. Vincent's Hospital after overdrinking at the White House Tavern in Greenwich Village?

A. Dylan Thomas.

Q. Poet Edgar Allan Poe was inspired to write "The Bells" by the church bells in what neighborhood?

A. Greenwich Village.

Q. What urbanite from New York edited *The Country Gentleman* magazine in the early 1900s?

A. Barton Wood Currie.

Q. If you are an unrecognized sculptor, at what self-service exhibition site in Queens can you display your work?

A. Socrates Park.

Lower Manhattan

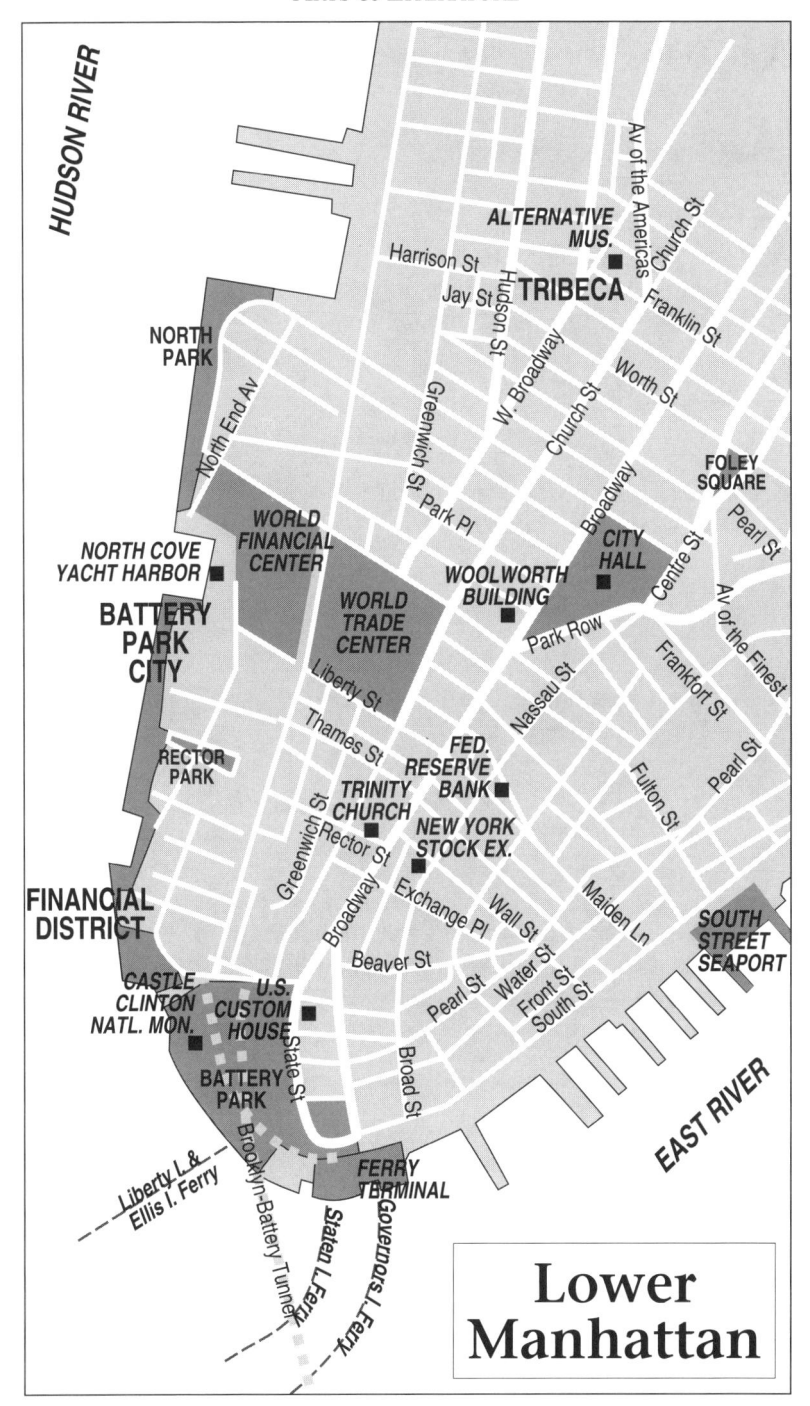

ARTS & LITERATURE

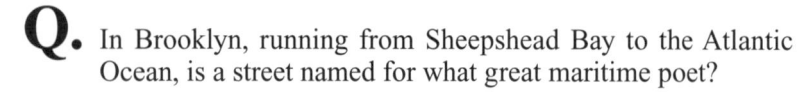

Q. In Brooklyn, running from Sheepshead Bay to the Atlantic Ocean, is a street named for what great maritime poet?

A. Samuel Taylor Coleridge.

Q. Who won the 1946 Caldecott Medal for writing the children's book that has been a bestseller ever since, *My Mother Is the Most Beautiful Woman in the World*?

A. Ruth Gannett.

Q. Near whose statue in Central Park are there regular readings of stories for children?

A. Hans Christian Andersen.

Q. What was the real name of Weegee, photographer of New York street life in the 1940s?

A. Arthur Fellig, who was portrayed by Joe Pesci in the 1992 film *The Public Eye*.

Q. Who designed the Guggenheim Museum on Fifth Avenue, between Eighty-eighth and Eighty-ninth Streets?

A. Frank Lloyd Wright.

Q. An original aim of the Guggenheim Museum was to exhibit and popularize what abstract painter?

A. Wassily Kandinsky.

Q. Where is the largest Picasso in town?

A. The lobby of the Seagram Building.

Arts & Literature

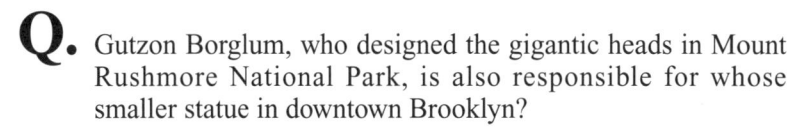

Q. Gutzon Borglum, who designed the gigantic heads in Mount Rushmore National Park, is also responsible for whose smaller statue in downtown Brooklyn?

A. The Reverend Henry Ward Beecher (1813–87), famed as an orator and lecturer.

Q. A dramatic version of Harriet Beecher Stowe's *Uncle Tom's Cabin* opened in 1852 at what Bowery theater?

A. Purdy's National.

Q. Thanks to what prolific diarist have the city's social and political events of the mid-nineteenth century been preserved?

A. George Templeton Strong (1820–75).

Q. What two gentlemen of Japan designed their country's cultural center in New York, Japan House at 333 East Forty-seventh Street?

A. Junzo Yoshimura and George Shimamoto.

Q. Instead of traveling to Russia, you can see the designs for Rimsky-Korsakov's operas at what museum that also displays an elaborate samovar?

A. The Nicholas Roerich Museum at 319 West 107th Street.

Q. What photographer has devoted his life to capturing the look and feel of the people and streets of Harlem?

A. James Van Der Zee.

Q. If America has become a kinder and gentler place, it may be because what ethicist was born in Brooklyn on July 31, 1943?

A. William J. Bennett.

Arts & Literature

Q. With the ongoing destruction of Tibetan culture by China, what institution has been a principal source for the study of its art and literature?

A. The Jacques Marchais Museum of Tibetan Art, 338 Lighthouse Avenue, Staten Island.

Q. What local bookstores specialize in mysteries?

A. Murder Ink (2486 Broadway) and Mysterious Book Shop (129 West Fifty-sixth Street).

Q. The first comic book was published in 1904 by what New York company?

A. Cupples & Leon.

Q. What was the most popular comic book published by Cupples & Leon?

A. *The Katzenjammer Kids.*

Q. What is the address of the only New York building designed by Louis Sullivan, founder of modern architecture in America?

A. 65 Bleecker Street.

Q. In what style of architecture is the seventy-seven-story Chrysler Building at 405 Lexington Avenue?

A. Art Deco.

Q. Cooper Union, opened in 1859 and dedicated to the education of working people, was paid for by what inventor-industrialist?

A. Peter Cooper.

Arts & Literature

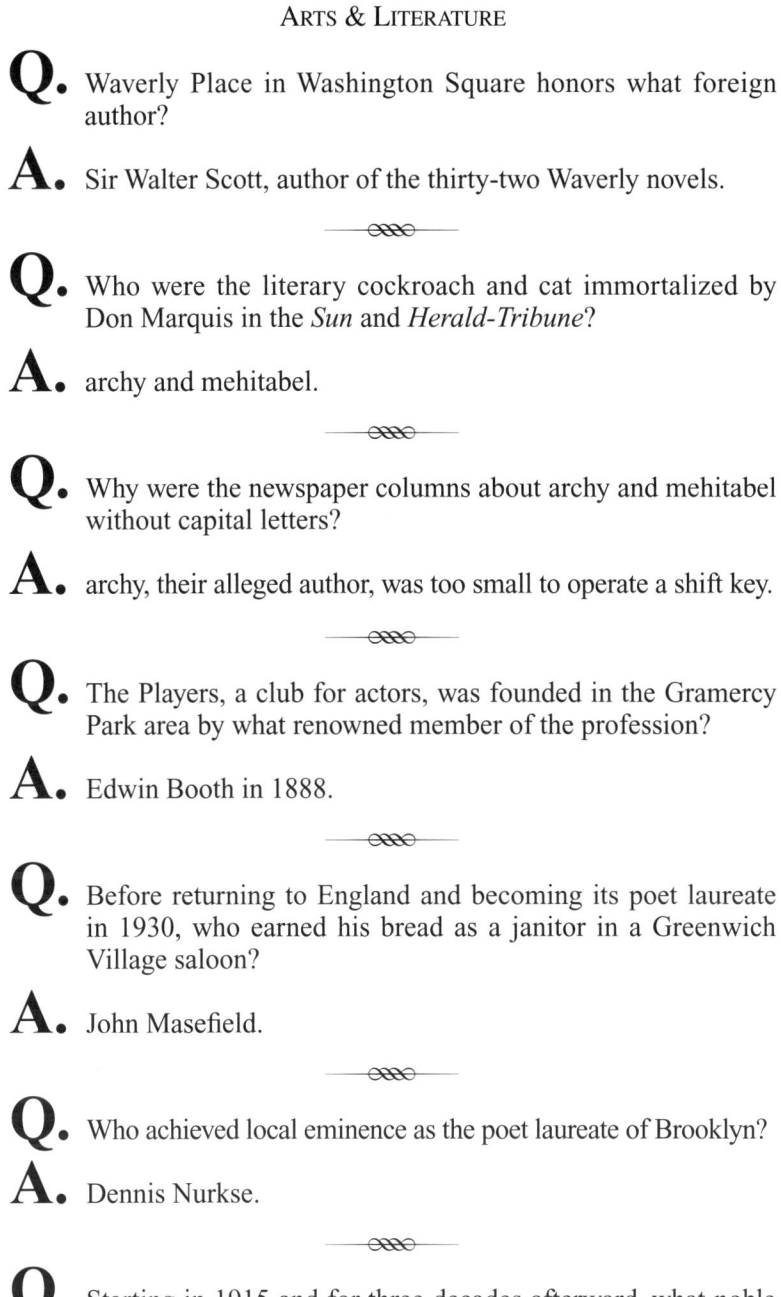

Q. Waverly Place in Washington Square honors what foreign author?

A. Sir Walter Scott, author of the thirty-two Waverly novels.

Q. Who were the literary cockroach and cat immortalized by Don Marquis in the *Sun* and *Herald-Tribune*?

A. archy and mehitabel.

Q. Why were the newspaper columns about archy and mehitabel without capital letters?

A. archy, their alleged author, was too small to operate a shift key.

Q. The Players, a club for actors, was founded in the Gramercy Park area by what renowned member of the profession?

A. Edwin Booth in 1888.

Q. Before returning to England and becoming its poet laureate in 1930, who earned his bread as a janitor in a Greenwich Village saloon?

A. John Masefield.

Q. Who achieved local eminence as the poet laureate of Brooklyn?

A. Dennis Nurkse.

Q. Starting in 1915 and for three decades afterward, what noble actor offered free theatrical classics to the poor?

A. Butler Davenport at the Davenport Theater, 138 East Twenty-seventh Street.

Arts & Literature

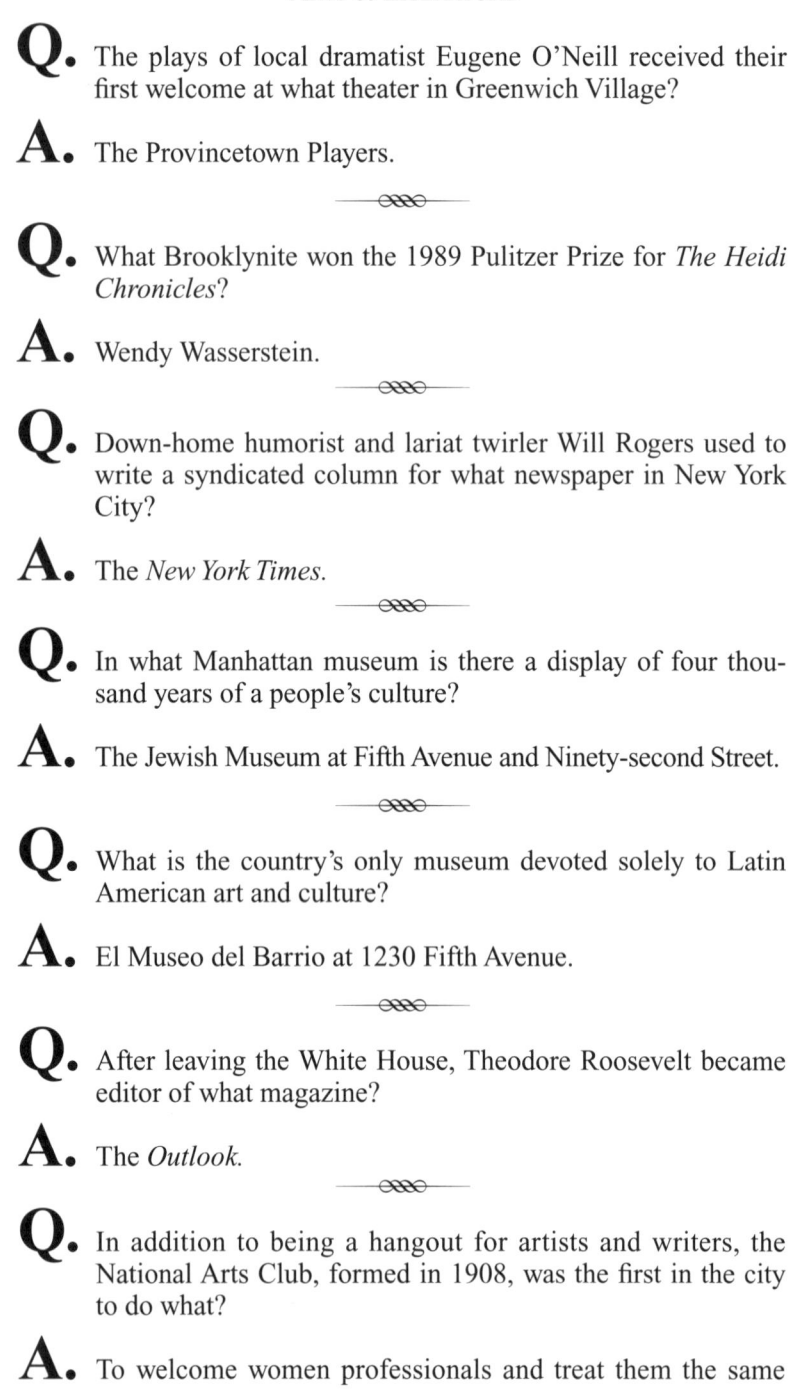

Q. The plays of local dramatist Eugene O'Neill received their first welcome at what theater in Greenwich Village?

A. The Provincetown Players.

Q. What Brooklynite won the 1989 Pulitzer Prize for *The Heidi Chronicles*?

A. Wendy Wasserstein.

Q. Down-home humorist and lariat twirler Will Rogers used to write a syndicated column for what newspaper in New York City?

A. The *New York Times*.

Q. In what Manhattan museum is there a display of four thousand years of a people's culture?

A. The Jewish Museum at Fifth Avenue and Ninety-second Street.

Q. What is the country's only museum devoted solely to Latin American art and culture?

A. El Museo del Barrio at 1230 Fifth Avenue.

Q. After leaving the White House, Theodore Roosevelt became editor of what magazine?

A. The *Outlook*.

Q. In addition to being a hangout for artists and writers, the National Arts Club, formed in 1908, was the first in the city to do what?

A. To welcome women professionals and treat them the same as men.

Arts & Literature

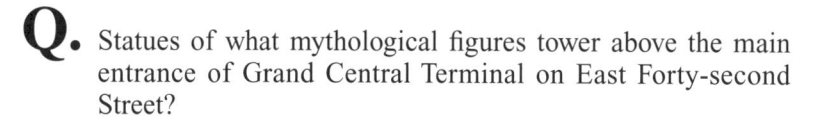

Q. Statues of what mythological figures tower above the main entrance of Grand Central Terminal on East Forty-second Street?

A. Minerva, Mercury, and Hercules.

Q. In the Rose Room restaurant of the Algonquin Hotel, what is the historic piece of furniture associated with actors and writers?

A. A round table.

Q. What was the best quip of Algonquin Round Table regular Alexander Woollcott?

A. "All the things I really like to do are either immoral, illegal, or fattening."

Q. Author Dorothy Parker, an Algonquin Round Table regular, suggested what epitaph for herself?

A. "Excuse my dust."

Q. James Thurber and E. B. White collaborated on what essential guide to living in New York and elsewhere?

A. *Is Sex Necessary? Or Why You Feel the Way You Do.*

Q. What was the first theater devoted to newsreels instead of entertainment films?

A. The Embassy in Times Square.

Q. Which of Mae West's plays was banned in 1921?

A. *Sex.*

Arts & Literature

Q. In 1921, Mae West spent how many days in jail for an indecent performance—theatrical, that is?

A. Ten.

Q. What was Mae West's principal complaint about jail?

A. Scratchy underwear. After her release, she told off the warden in a poem.

Q. Though her biggest stage and screen role was as Diamond Lil, in what costume-jewelry part of Brooklyn was Mae West born?

A. Greenpoint.

Q. To which actor did Mae West display friendliness and say, "Why don't you come up sometime and see me?"

A. Cary Grant.

Q. What Episcopal church on Park Avenue at East Fiftieth Street is in a style of Byzantine architecture that you would expect to see in Istanbul?

A. St. Bartholomew's.

Q. The architecture of what synagogue building, the oldest in town, has been compared to a Gothic cathedral in Cologne?

A. Built in 1849, Anshe Chesed at 172 Norfolk Street on the Lower East Side.

Q. The Grolier Club (47 East Sixtieth Street), founded in 1884 and dedicated to the production and exhibition of fine books, is named for whom?

A. Jean Grolier, a sixteenth-century French bibliophile.

Arts & Literature

The New York Public Library, with more than 49 million cultural treasures, is now considered one of the five greatest libraries in the world.
New York Convention and Visitors Bureau.

Q. Andrew Carnegie was the principal benefactor of what other cultural amenity in the city?

A. The public library system.

Q. When was the New York Public Library established?

A. In 1895.

Q. In which novel by F. Scott Fitzgerald do characters hang out at the Plaza Hotel?

A. *The Great Gatsby.*

Q. To what radio stations do New Yorkers dial for classical music?

A. WNYC-FM and WQXR.

Arts & Literature

Q. Where on the dial can New Yorkers hear country music?

A. WGSM, WMJC, and WRGX.

Q. After leaving Scotland, what master furniture maker opened a shop on Fulton Street in the early 1790s?

A. Duncan Phyfe.

Q. What is the name of the mural in the bar at the St. Regis Hotel?

A. *Old King Cole.* It was painted by Maxfield Parrish.

Q. In "The Gift of the Magi" by O. Henry, what do Della and Jim, indigent New Yorkers, exchange at Christmas?

A. A watch fob and combs.

Q. In Theodore Dreiser's first novel, which of his gallery of tragic heroines comes to New York in search of living the American Dream of wealth, success, and love?

A. Sister Carrie.

Q. On the first page of a novel about New York and America, what European author describes the Statue of Liberty as holding a sword rather than a torch?

A. Franz Kafka in *Amerika*.

Q. In 1850, what foreign singer made a New York debut almost as sensational as the Beatles' in 1964?

A. Jenny Lind, the Swedish Nightingale.

ARTS & LITERATURE

Q. What two-time Pulitzer Prize winner in history had no college degree in the subject?

A. Barbara Tuchman.

Q. The King of Mambo is and will always be what New Yorker?

A. Tito Puente.

Q. Tito Puente used to play his mambos, bossa novas, and cha-chas at what dance hall on Broadway?

A. The Palladium.

Q. What elaborate building at the corner of Lafayette and East Houston Streets has a Shakespeare character over the doorway?

A. The Puck Building, finished in 1899.

Q. In the early part of the twentieth century, what ensemble gave free concerts at Central and Prospect Parks?

A. The Goldman Band.

Q. A bust of what great composer stares at the shell where musicians perform in Central Park?

A. Beethoven.

Q. Scottish-American industrialist Andrew Carnegie, who financed the building of Carnegie Hall in 1891, preferred what kind of music?

A. Bagpipes.

Arts & Literature

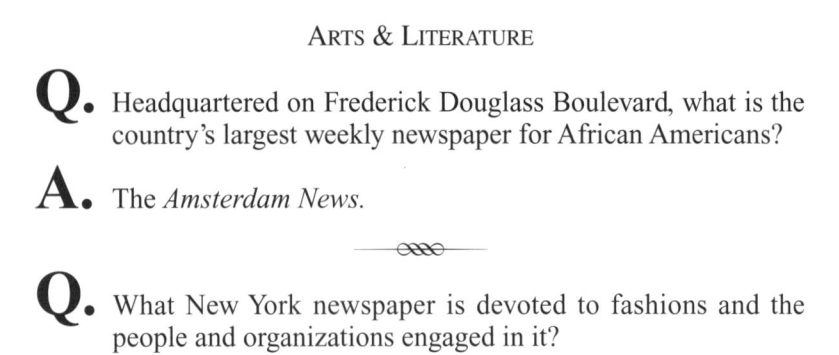

Q. Headquartered on Frederick Douglass Boulevard, what is the country's largest weekly newspaper for African Americans?

A. The *Amsterdam News*.

Q. What New York newspaper is devoted to fashions and the people and organizations engaged in it?

A. *Women's Wear Daily*.

Q. The Brooklyn Public Library, which began operations under that name in 1897, was founded under what other name in 1853?

A. The Brooklyn Athenaeum Reading Room.

Q. *The Sheltering Sky* is by what local novelist who preferred to be sheltered by the sky over North Africa?

A. Paul Bowles.

Q. Marianne Moore never won a fashion prize for her famous tricorne hat, but what prize did she win in 1952 for *Collected Poems*?

A. The Pulitzer Prize.

Q. In 1980, suspense novelist Mary Higgins Clark began her avalanche of bestsellers with what two mysteries about youngsters?

A. *Where Are the Children?* and *The Cradle Will Fall*.

Q. What great composer died in a mental hospital on Ward's Island in 1917?

A. Scott Joplin.

Arts & Literature

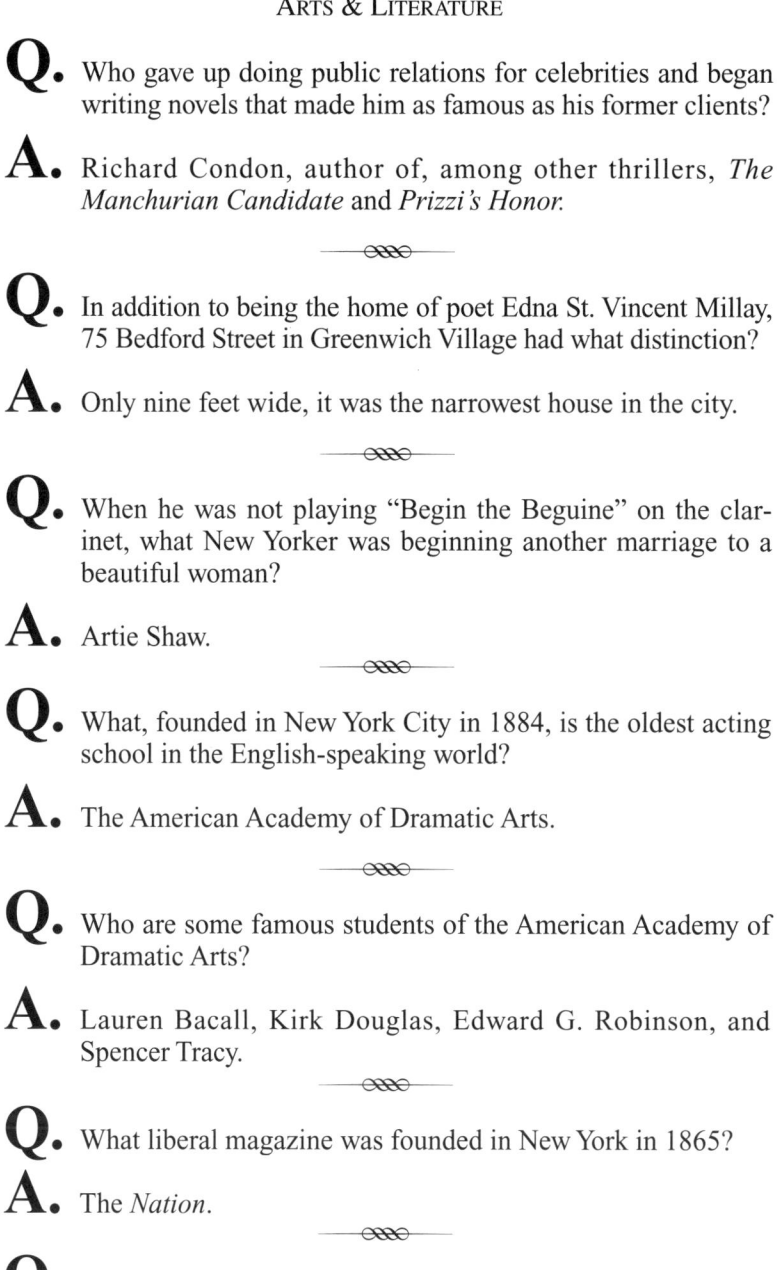

Q. Who gave up doing public relations for celebrities and began writing novels that made him as famous as his former clients?

A. Richard Condon, author of, among other thrillers, *The Manchurian Candidate* and *Prizzi's Honor.*

Q. In addition to being the home of poet Edna St. Vincent Millay, 75 Bedford Street in Greenwich Village had what distinction?

A. Only nine feet wide, it was the narrowest house in the city.

Q. When he was not playing "Begin the Beguine" on the clarinet, what New Yorker was beginning another marriage to a beautiful woman?

A. Artie Shaw.

Q. What, founded in New York City in 1884, is the oldest acting school in the English-speaking world?

A. The American Academy of Dramatic Arts.

Q. Who are some famous students of the American Academy of Dramatic Arts?

A. Lauren Bacall, Kirk Douglas, Edward G. Robinson, and Spencer Tracy.

Q. What liberal magazine was founded in New York in 1865?

A. The *Nation*.

Q. In between his other chores in the Archdiocese of New York, Cardinal Francis Spellman wrote what best-selling novel in 1951?

A. *The Foundling.*

Arts & Literature

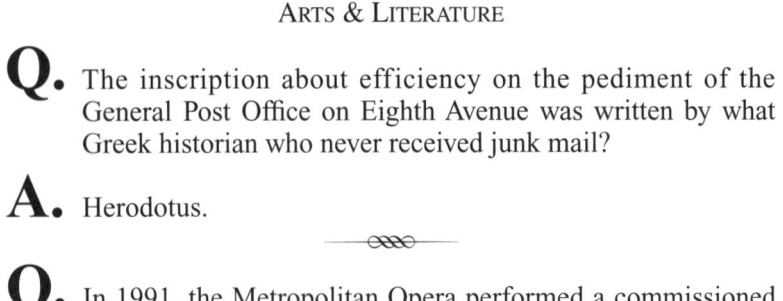

Q. The inscription about efficiency on the pediment of the General Post Office on Eighth Avenue was written by what Greek historian who never received junk mail?

A. Herodotus.

Q. In 1991, the Metropolitan Opera performed a commissioned work by what Italian American who was following in the footsteps of Verdi and Puccini?

A. John Corigliano, who wrote *The Ghosts of Versailles*.

Q. *The Metropolitan Opera Murders* was written by what Wagnerian soprano who never committed a worse crime than punctured eardrums during her career at the Met?

A. Helen Traubel.

Q. Opera star Helen Traubel was a frequent guest and second banana on the radio program of what local comedian?

A. Jimmy Durante.

Q. What Staten Islander was a choreographer and director of the Joffrey Ballet?

A. Gerald Arpino.

Q. Who, now honored as an early master of photography, did not receive recognition until old age?

A. Alice Austen (1866–1952) of Staten Island.

Q. After defecting from the Soviet Union, Mikhail Baryshnikov performed with what two dance companies?

A. American Ballet Theater and the New York City Ballet.

Arts & Literature

Q. What Brooklyn church contains paintings by Vatican artist Francesco Galliardi?

A. St. Teresa of Avila Roman Catholic Church at 563 Sterling Place.

Q. In 1949, what Brooklynite won an Oscar for his music score about a wealthy New York family with romantic problems?

A. Aaron Copland for *The Heiress.*

Q. Greenwich Villager Stephen Crane, author of *The Red Badge of Courage,* wrote what novel about the city's slums?

A. *Maggie: A Girl of the Streets* published in 1893.

Q. In 1914, what organization was formed to protect the commercial rights of creative artists?

A. The American Society of Composers, Authors, and Publishers (ASCAP, for short).

Q. Who founded the New York Civic Repertory Theater in 1926?

A. Eva Le Gallienne.

Q. Eva Le Gallienne, founder of the Civic Repertory Theater, refused to admit what later Oscar winner to her acting school?

A. Bette Davis.

Q. Who, in 1921, was the first cartoonist to win a Pulitzer Prize?

A. Rollin Kirby of the *World.*

Arts & Literature

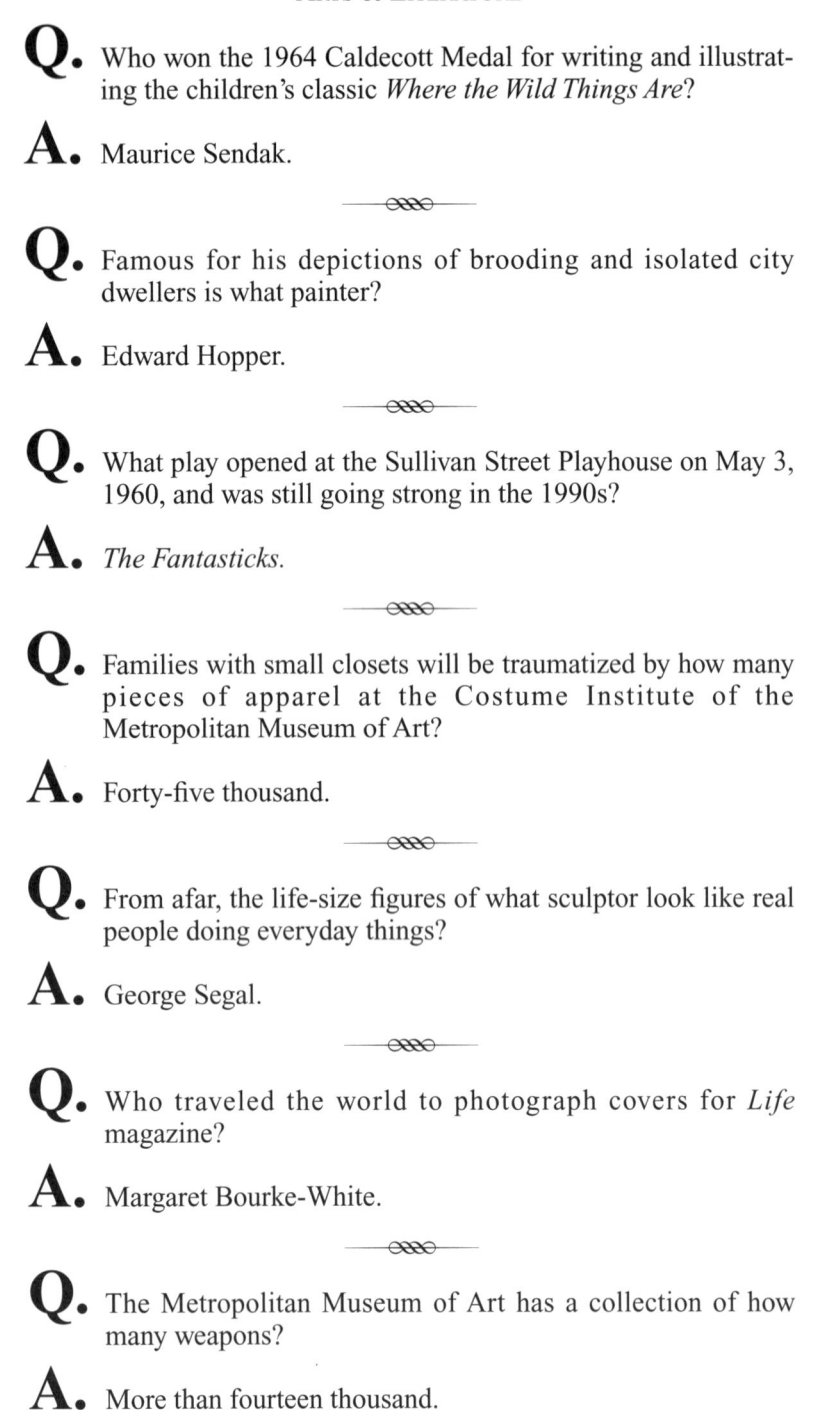

Q. Who won the 1964 Caldecott Medal for writing and illustrating the children's classic *Where the Wild Things Are*?

A. Maurice Sendak.

Q. Famous for his depictions of brooding and isolated city dwellers is what painter?

A. Edward Hopper.

Q. What play opened at the Sullivan Street Playhouse on May 3, 1960, and was still going strong in the 1990s?

A. *The Fantasticks.*

Q. Families with small closets will be traumatized by how many pieces of apparel at the Costume Institute of the Metropolitan Museum of Art?

A. Forty-five thousand.

Q. From afar, the life-size figures of what sculptor look like real people doing everyday things?

A. George Segal.

Q. Who traveled the world to photograph covers for *Life* magazine?

A. Margaret Bourke-White.

Q. The Metropolitan Museum of Art has a collection of how many weapons?

A. More than fourteen thousand.

SPORTS & LEISURE

CHAPTER FIVE

*Girls and boys, come out to play,
The moon doth shine as bright as day.
Leave your supper and leave your sleep,
And come with your playfellows into the street.*
—Mother Goose

Q. What is the city's oldest park?

A. Bowling Green, established March 12, 1733.

Q. What was the favorite sport of the Dutch who inhabited early New York?

A. Bowling.

Q. Who, the son of a slave, was America's first international sports hero?

A. Boxer Bill Richmond of Staten Island, who was born August 5, 1763.

Q. What is the oldest canoe club in the country?

A. The New York Canoe Club, established in 1871.

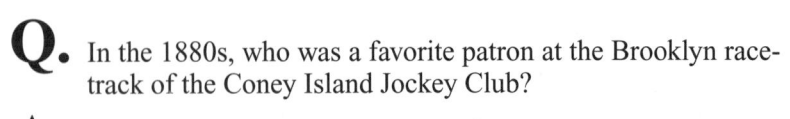

Q. In the 1880s, who was a favorite patron at the Brooklyn racetrack of the Coney Island Jockey Club?

A. John W. "Bet a Million" Gates.

Q. What two sports greats gave free lessons at the World's Fair of 1939?

A. Babe Ruth and Jack Dempsey.

Q. To what sport is the Polar Bear Club dedicated?

A. Wintertime swimming in the Atlantic Ocean off Coney Island.

Q. Who devised the rules of baseball in 1846?

A. Alexander J. Cartwright Jr.

Q. The National Baseball League was organized in 1876 in what hotel?

A. The Broadway Central.

Q. When did a New York City club, the Knickerbockers, play the first game of baseball?

A. June 19, 1846.

Q. When did a New York team first win a World Series?

A. The Giants in 1905.

Sports & Leisure

Q. What was the nickname of the New York Yankees until recent years?

A. The Bronx Bombers.

Q. When a Yankee made an error, how did fans express disapproval?

A. With a Bronx cheer, which is a vulgar and derisive sound made by blowing across the tongue.

Q. For what catch phrase is Willie Mays of the Giants remembered?

A. "Say, hey!"

Q. After a sensational play, what was the inevitable comment of Yankee announcer Mel Allen?

A. "How 'bout that?"

Q. Mel Allen and who else were the first announcers inducted into the Baseball Hall of Fame?

A. Dodger and Yankee announcer Red Barber.

Q. For what paper was Red Smith writing when he won the 1976 Pulitzer Prize for his sports coverage?

A. The *New York Times*.

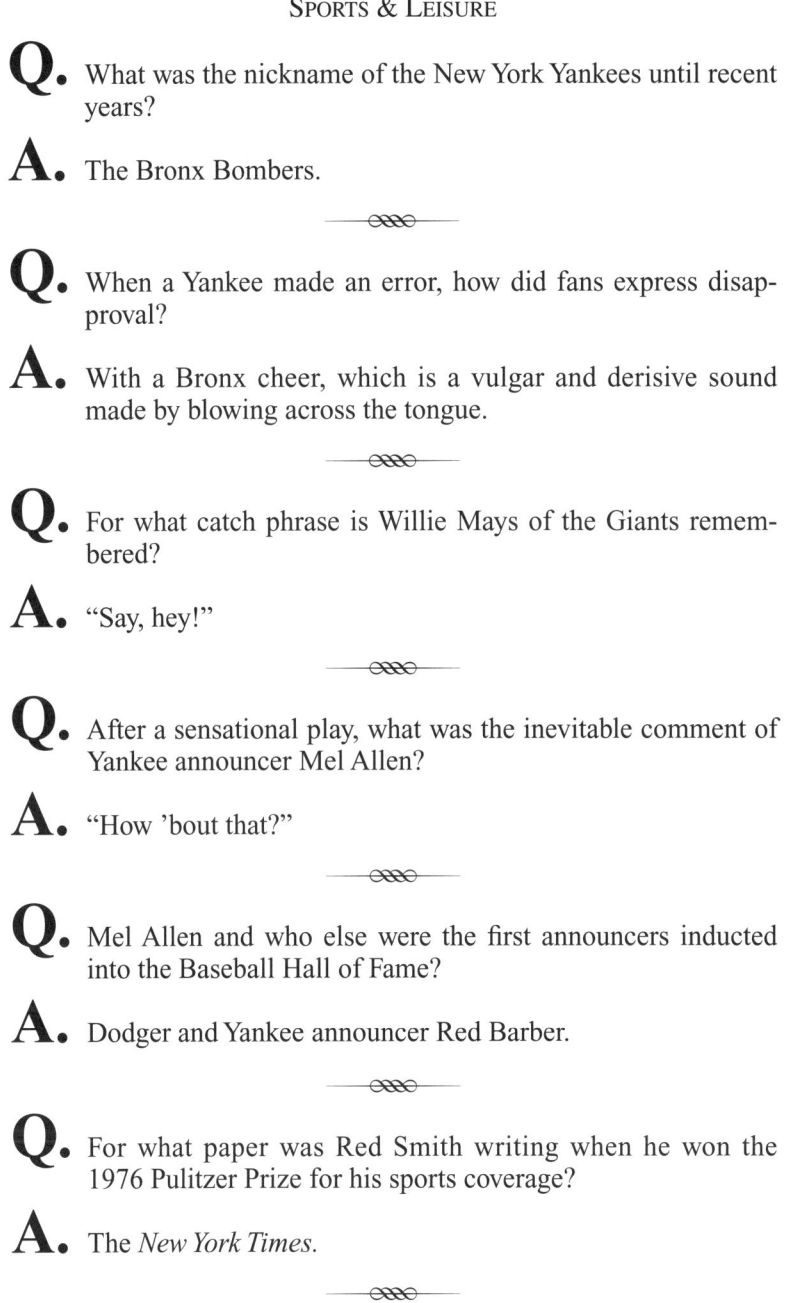

Q. Who said, "It ain't over till it's over"?

A. Yogi Berra.

Q. What team represented New York in the National Colored Base Ball League, founded in 1887?

A. The Gorhams.

Q. Tap dancer Bill "Bojangles" Robinson formed what African-American baseball team in 1931?

A. New York Black Yankees.

Q. Where, on August 26, 1939, was the first telecast of a major-league baseball game?

A. Ebbets Field in Brooklyn.

Q. Where, on February 28, 1940, was the first telecast of a basketball game?

A. Madison Square Garden.

Q. Who managed the Brooklyn Dodgers to their first world championship in 1955?

A. Walt Alston.

Q. What was the nickname of the Brooklyn Dodgers?

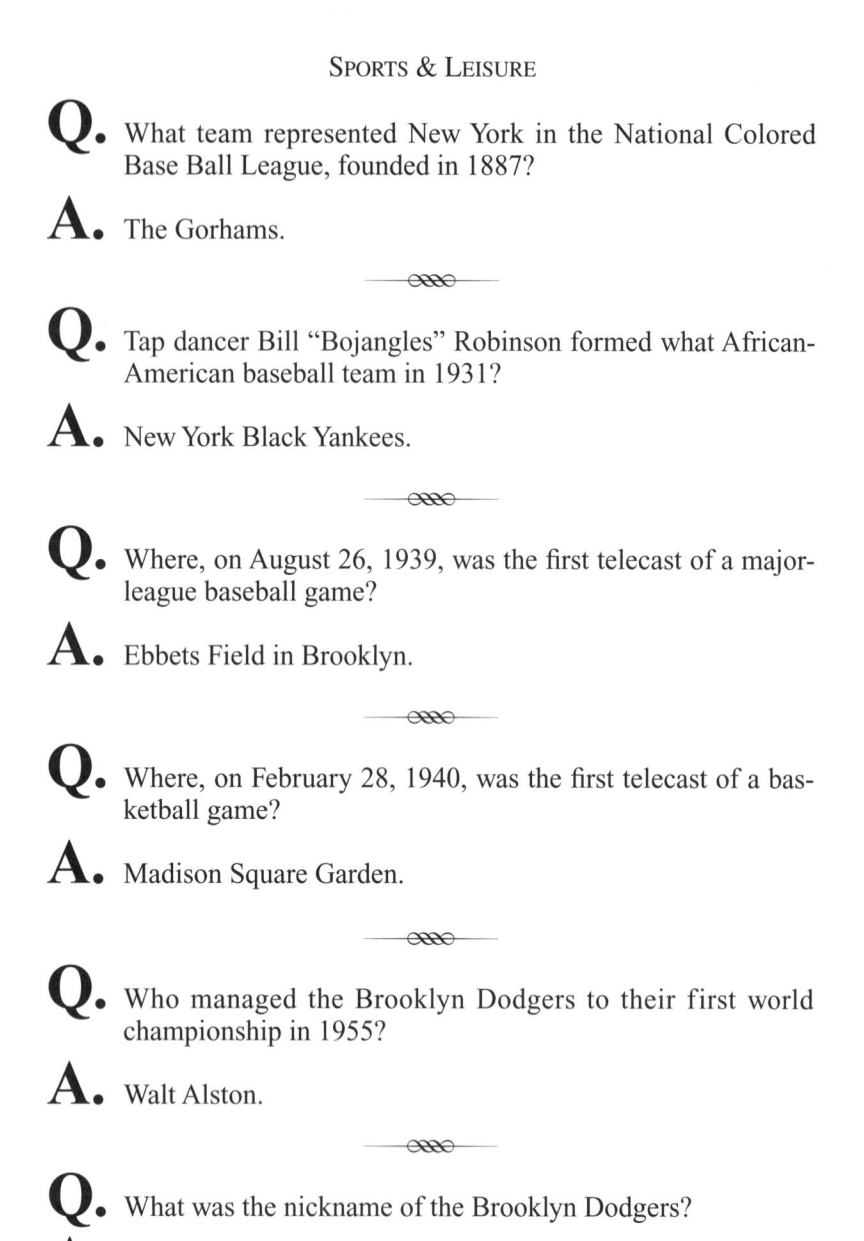

A. Dem Bums.

Q. Whether their team won or lost, what did Dodger fans call themselves?

A. The Flatbush Faithful.

SPORTS & LEISURE

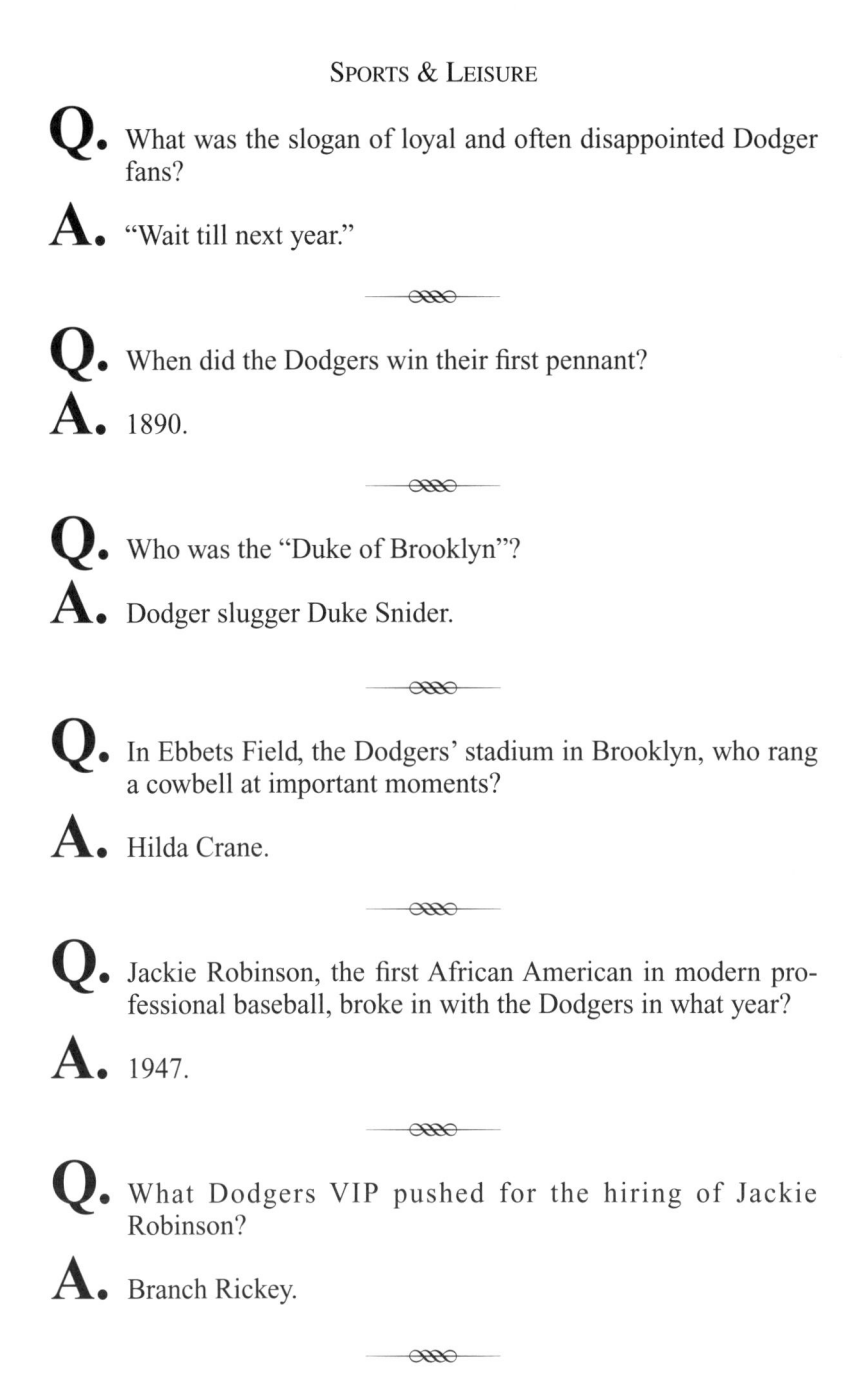

Q. What was the slogan of loyal and often disappointed Dodger fans?

A. "Wait till next year."

Q. When did the Dodgers win their first pennant?

A. 1890.

Q. Who was the "Duke of Brooklyn"?

A. Dodger slugger Duke Snider.

Q. In Ebbets Field, the Dodgers' stadium in Brooklyn, who rang a cowbell at important moments?

A. Hilda Crane.

Q. Jackie Robinson, the first African American in modern professional baseball, broke in with the Dodgers in what year?

A. 1947.

Q. What Dodgers VIP pushed for the hiring of Jackie Robinson?

A. Branch Rickey.

Q. What Dodger won three MVP Awards during the 1950s?

A. Catcher and slugger Roy Campanella.

Sports & Leisure

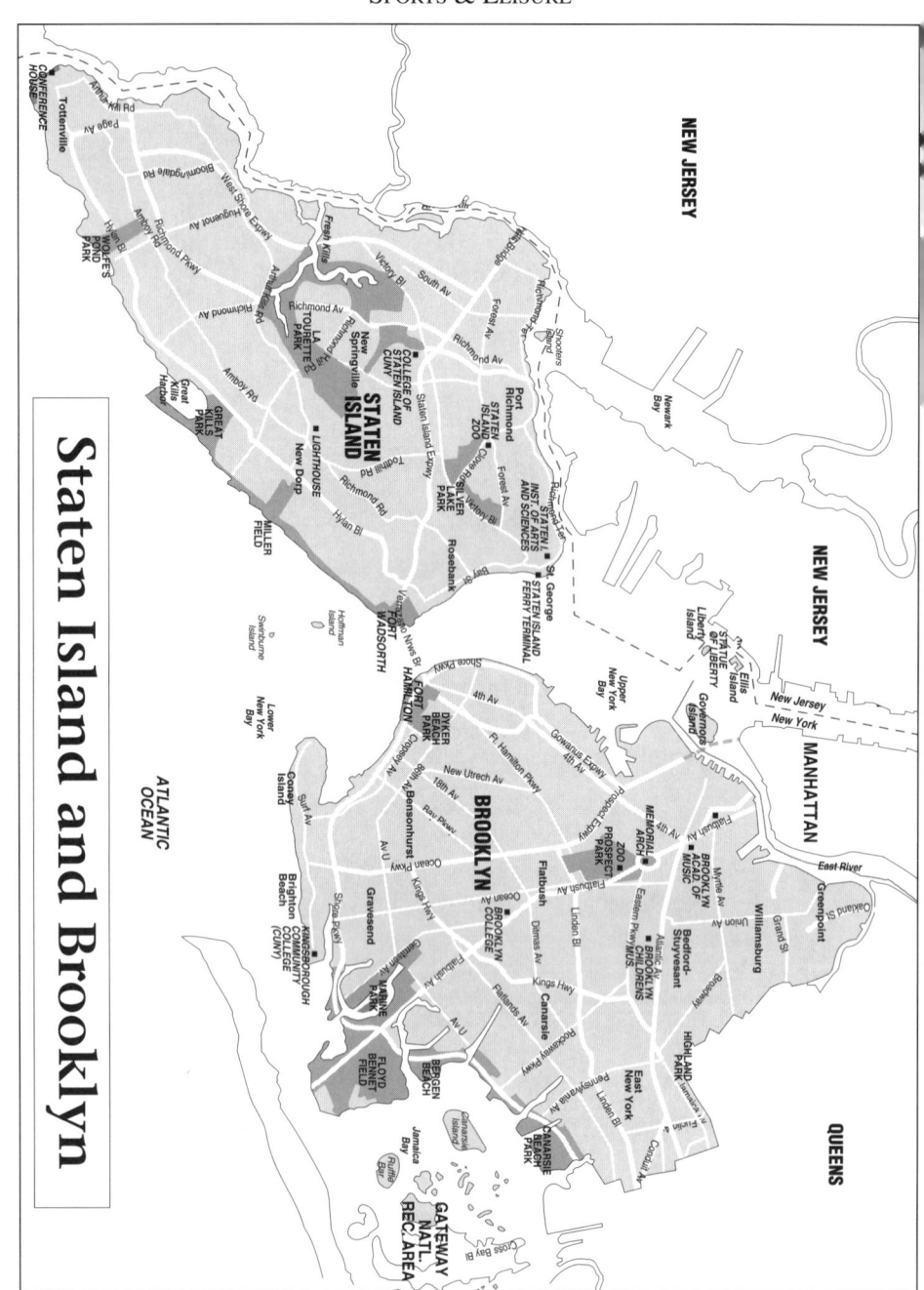

Staten Island and Brooklyn

Sports & Leisure

Q. The Brooklyn Dodgers once had what other names?

A. Superbas, Robins, Kings, and Bridegrooms.

Q. Brooklyn sports fans had to endure what trauma on October 8, 1957?

A. The Dodgers deserted them for a foreign place called Los Angeles.

Q. When was the Dodgers' last game in Brooklyn?

A. September 24, 1957.

Q. Who was the first Dodger picked for an All-Star Game?

A. Second baseman Tony Cuccinello in 1933.

Q. In the first All-Star Game, held in 1933, what Yankee was the winning pitcher?

A. Lefty Gomez.

Q. When and where did New York host its first All-Star Game?

A. 1934 at the Polo Grounds.

Q. Who, in 1951, was the first New York Giant to pitch the National League to victory in an All-Star Game?

A. Sal Maglie, aka the Barber.

Sports & Leisure

Q. What so-so player acquired fame as the Clown Prince of Baseball?

A. Al Schacht.

Q. Who invented four-wheel roller skates?

A. James L. Plimpton in 1863.

Q. What chess organization was founded in the city in 1857?

A. The American Chess Association.

Q. Who, in 1896, set out from Battery Park and crossed the Atlantic in a rowboat?

A. George Harpo and Frank Samuelson.

Q. What was the first rowing club in the country?

A. Castle Garden Amateur Boat Club Association in 1834.

Q. With the popularity of television and the proliferation of couch potatoes in the 1960s, who encouraged the country to get out there and start jogging?

A. Jim Fixx, runner and author of the best-selling *Complete Book of Jogging.*

Q. Why was track star John Carlos expelled from the 1968 Olympic Games?

A. On the winner's stand, he had raised his fists to protest racial discrimination.

Sports & Leisure

Q. In what year did Yankee Stadium open?
A. 1923.

Q. Having trained the winners of 2,275 races, James E. Fitzsimmons bore what nickname that expressed his optimism about his horses?
A. Sunny Jim.

Q. In 1922, who played in the first World Series that was broadcast play by play?
A. The Giants and the Yankees.

Q. When did major-league night baseball begin in the city?
A. June 15, 1938.

Q. In what years did Joe McCarthy lead the Yanks to glory?
A. From 1931 to 1946.

Q. The Yankees have won how many World Series?
A. Twenty-three, as of 1996.

Q. What Yankee sluggers comprised Murderers Row during the 1927 season?
A. Babe Ruth, Lou Gehrig, Bob Meusel, and Tony Lazzeri.

Q. During their great years in the 1930s, the Yankees were owned by what local brewer?

A. Col. Jacob Ruppert.

Q. Who holds the record for hits in the World Series?

A. Yogi Berra of the Yankees had seventy-one.

Q. Who holds the World Series record for homers?

A. Yankee slugger Mickey Mantle hit eighteen.

Q. What was the achievement of Yankee hurler Allie Reynolds in 1951?

A. He pitched two no-hitters during the season.

Q. When did Yankee slugger Reggie Jackson enter the Hall of Fame?

A. 1993.

Q. In how many consecutive games did Joe DiMaggio, "the Yankee Clipper," get a hit in 1941?

A. Fifty-six.

Q. What two local players have won the Triple Crown for batting?

A. Lou Gehrig (1934) and Mickey Mantle (1956).

SPORTS & LEISURE

Q. In 1904, what local pitcher set an all-time season record of forty-one wins?

A. Jack Chesbro of the New York Highlanders, which became the Yankees in 1913.

Q. Who has pitched the most wins in a World Series?

A. Whitey Ford of the Yankees won ten games.

Q. Who holds the major-league record for grand-slam homers?

A. Lou Gehrig with twenty-three.

Q. Lou Gehrig, baseball's "Iron Horse," played in how many consecutive games as a Yankee?

A. 2,130.

Q. Gehrig succeeded what other player at first base?

A. Wally Pipp.

Q. In what year did Roger Maris hit his sixty-one homers?

A. 1961.

Q. In what year did Babe Ruth hit sixty homers?

A. 1927.

Sports & Leisure

Q. When did Yogi Berra manage the New York Mets?
A. From 1972 to 1975.

Q. In what year did the Mets start to play in Shea Stadium?
A. 1964.

Q. When did Casey Stengel manage the Mets?
A. From 1962 to 1965.

Q. With what names did his parents christen Casey Stengel?
A. Charles Dillon.

Q. To how many victories did Casey Stengel lead the Yankees?
A. Ten pennants and seven World Series.

Q. Where can fans see Casey's old Dodger uniform?
A. The Brooklyn Historical Society at 128 Pierrepont Street.

Q. What New York book publisher became the majority owner of the Mets in 1980?
A. Nelson Doubleday.

Sports & Leisure

Q. Under whose leadership did the Giants win ten National League championships and three World Series?

A. Hall of Famer John J. McGraw who managed them from 1903 to 1932.

Q. Who succeeded John J. McGraw as Giants manager?

A. Bill Terry.

Q. Who was the "Old Meal Ticket" of the New York Giants?

A. Southpaw pitcher Carl Hubbell.

Q. Carl Hubbell holds a major-league record for winning how many consecutive games?

A. Twenty-four.

Q. During the late 1930s, what St. Louis Cardinal slugger was Carl Hubbell's nemesis?

A. Joe "Ducky" Medwick.

Q. Andrew Freedman, an early owner of the Giants, displayed his civic spirit in what way?

A. He endowed a retirement home for the old and poor.

Q. In what year did the Giants leave town and start playing in San Francisco?

A. 1958.

Q. What player for a New York team pitched a no-hitter in which no one reached first base?

A. Yankee Don Larsen on October 8, 1956.

Q. Who was the last Brooklyn Dodger to win the MVP Award?

A. Don Newcombe in 1956.

Q. Who was the first and also the last Brooklyn pitcher to win the Cy Young Award?

A. Don Newcombe in 1956.

Q. Who was the first Yankee to win the Cy Young Award?

A. Bob Turley in 1958.

Q. Who was the first Met to win the Cy Young Award?

A. Tom Seaver in 1969.

Q. Until it folded in 1919, what was considered the fastest auto racing track in the world?

A. Sheepshead Speedway in Brooklyn.

Q. Who led the New York Jets to a Super Bowl victory in 1969?

A. Joe Namath.

Sports & Leisure

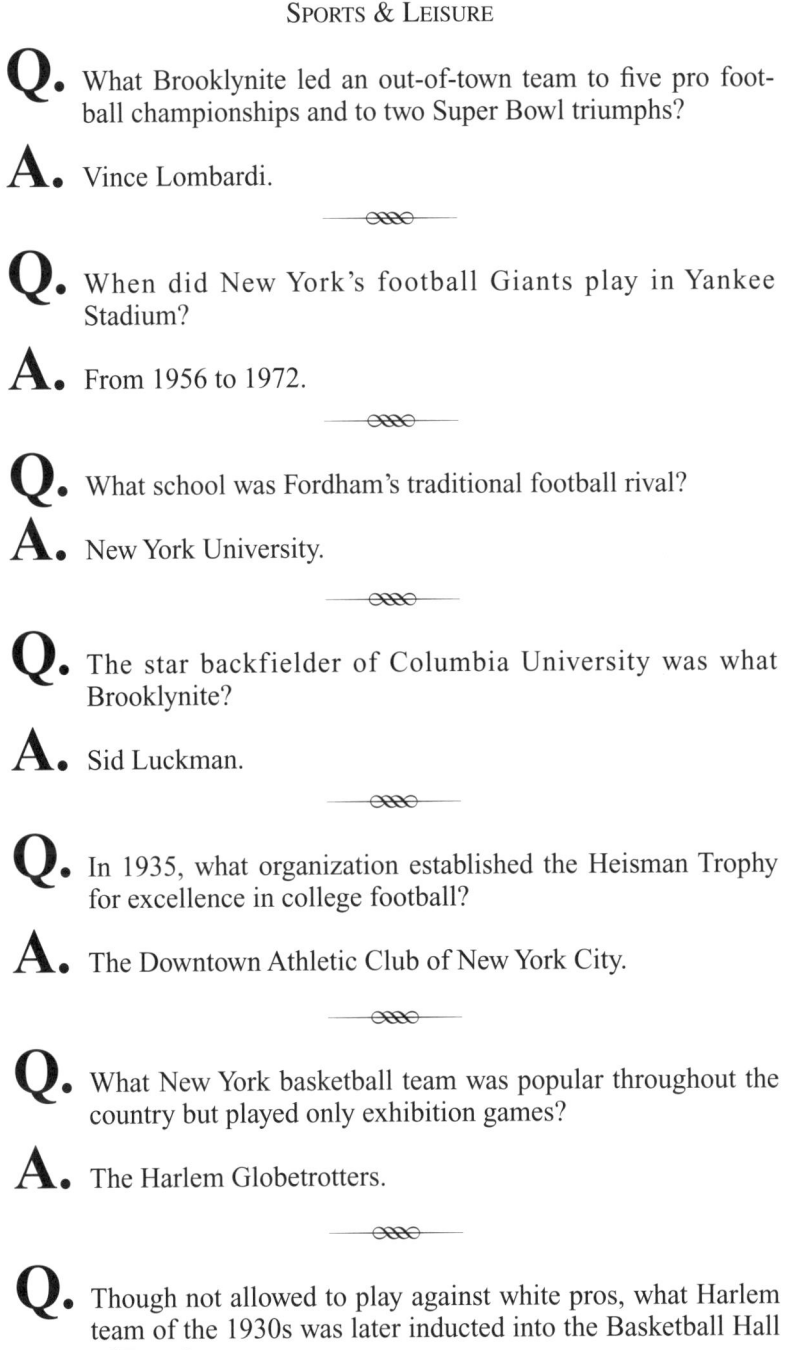

Q. What Brooklynite led an out-of-town team to five pro football championships and to two Super Bowl triumphs?

A. Vince Lombardi.

Q. When did New York's football Giants play in Yankee Stadium?

A. From 1956 to 1972.

Q. What school was Fordham's traditional football rival?

A. New York University.

Q. The star backfielder of Columbia University was what Brooklynite?

A. Sid Luckman.

Q. In 1935, what organization established the Heisman Trophy for excellence in college football?

A. The Downtown Athletic Club of New York City.

Q. What New York basketball team was popular throughout the country but played only exhibition games?

A. The Harlem Globetrotters.

Q. Though not allowed to play against white pros, what Harlem team of the 1930s was later inducted into the Basketball Hall of Fame?

A. The Rens.

Sports & Leisure

Q. What basketball player from Brooklyn led the "Dream Team" to a gold medal in the 1984 Olympic Games?

A. Michael Jordan.

Q. In March 1997, what star from Queens led Tennessee's Lady Vols to their second straight national title in women's basketball?

A. Chamique Holdsclaw.

Q. How tall was Barney Sedran, top City College of New York basketball scorer for three seasons and then a pro for fifteen years?

A. Five feet four inches tall.

Q. What four Jewish players from Brooklyn led St. John's University to basketball glory in the 1930s?

A. Rip Geyson, Mac Kinsbrunner, Max Posnak, and Allie Schuckman.

Q. What New Yorker was a four-time winner of the NBA's MVP Award?

A. Kareem Abdul-Jabbar.

Q. Who was an original Celtic and then a longtime coach for the City College of New York?

A. Nat Holman.

Q. Who was the first Knick to win the NBA's MVP Award?

A. Willis Reed in 1970.

Sports & Leisure

Q. Who led the Knicks to the top of their division and became NBA Coach of the Year in 1993?

A. Pat Riley.

Q. To what local racetrack do New Yorkers go?

A. Aqueduct in Queens.

Q. What former middleweight champ wrote a best-selling autobiography called *Somebody Up There Likes Me*?

A. Rocky Graziano.

Q. After hanging up his six-shooters, what gunfighter from the West became a sportswriter for the *New York Morning Telegraph* in 1902?

A. William Barclay Masterson, aka Bat Masterson.

Q. During the 1930s, what annual sports event covered even more ground than the current New York Marathon?

A. The Six-Day Bicycle Race.

Q. Held the first Sunday in May, what forty-two-mile race visits the five boroughs and is the longest event of its sort in the U.S.?

A. The Bike New York Tour, which started in 1977.

Q. In the 1930s, who participated in the changing of pro wrestling from an athletic competition to a theatrical event with comedy, heroes, and villains?

A. Man Mountain Dean.

Sports & Leisure

Q. Who was the Astoria Assassin?

A. Paul Berlenbach, world light heavyweight boxing champ from 1925 to 1933.

Q. What former boxing champ used to sit near the window of his Times Square restaurant and greet fans?

A. Jack Dempsey.

Q. Jack Dempsey lost his heavyweight title to what New Yorker?

A. Gene Tunney.

Q. Where did Maxie Rosenbloom and other local fighters train for their bouts at Madison Square Garden?

A. Stillman's Gym.

Q. Who refereed most of the big fights at the old Madison Square Garden on Eighth Avenue?

A. Arthur Donovan.

Q. What was the nickname of Jim Braddock, who upset Max Baer for boxing's heavyweight title in 1935?

A. The Cinderella Man.

Q. For New York children of all ages, what is the great spring event at Madison Square Garden?

A. The Ringling Brothers and Barnum & Bailey Circus.

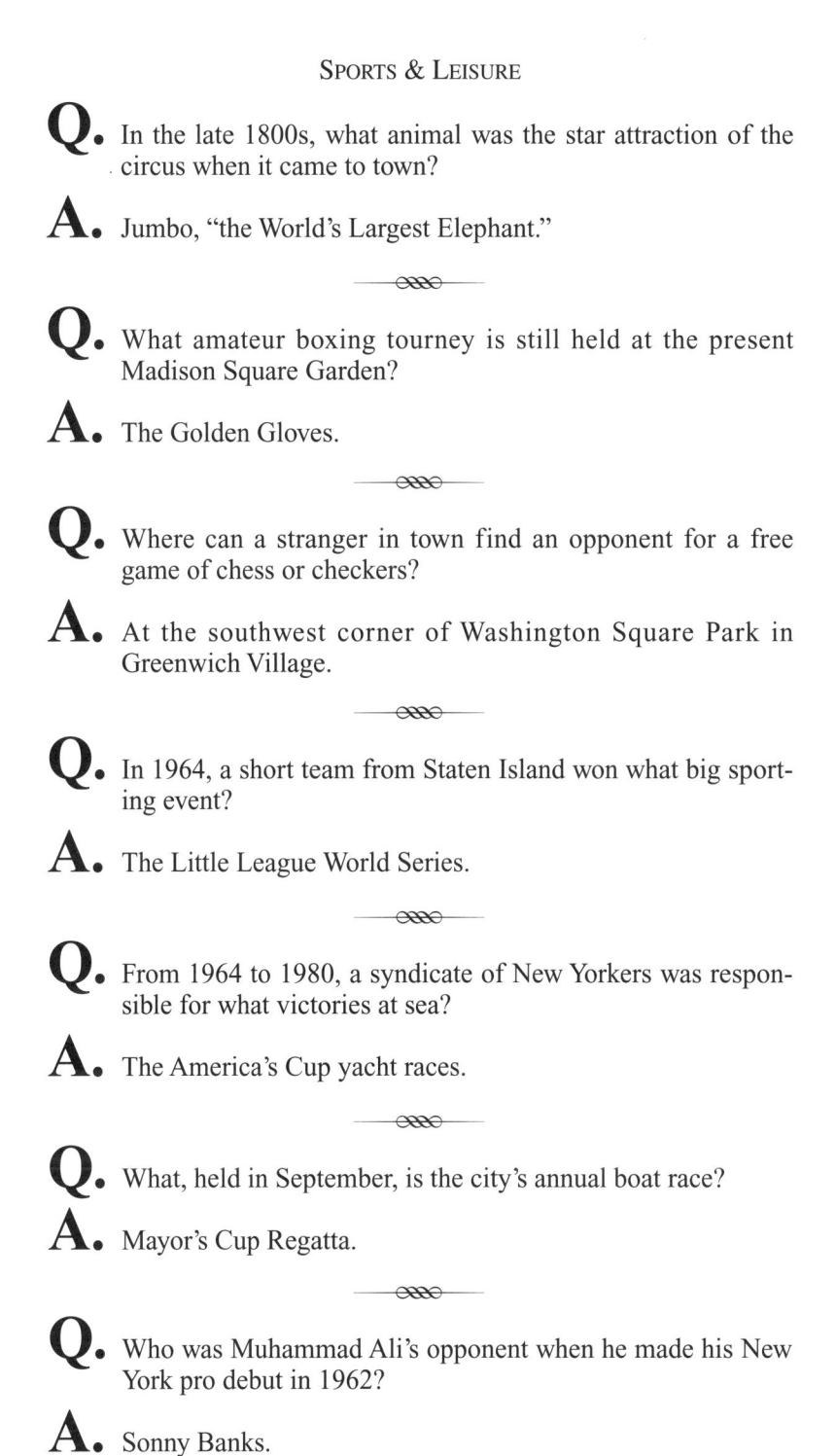

Sports & Leisure

Q. In the late 1800s, what animal was the star attraction of the circus when it came to town?

A. Jumbo, "the World's Largest Elephant."

Q. What amateur boxing tourney is still held at the present Madison Square Garden?

A. The Golden Gloves.

Q. Where can a stranger in town find an opponent for a free game of chess or checkers?

A. At the southwest corner of Washington Square Park in Greenwich Village.

Q. In 1964, a short team from Staten Island won what big sporting event?

A. The Little League World Series.

Q. From 1964 to 1980, a syndicate of New Yorkers was responsible for what victories at sea?

A. The America's Cup yacht races.

Q. What, held in September, is the city's annual boat race?

A. Mayor's Cup Regatta.

Q. Who was Muhammad Ali's opponent when he made his New York pro debut in 1962?

A. Sonny Banks.

Sports & Leisure

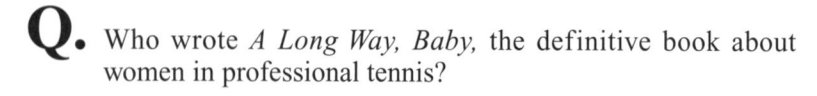

Q. Who wrote *A Long Way, Baby,* the definitive book about women in professional tennis?

A. Grace Lichtenstein.

Q. What tennis player from Harlem was Wimbledon champ in 1957?

A. Althea Gibson.

Q. Where is the U.S. Open Tennis Championship held?

A. The National Tennis Center at Flushing Meadows in Queens.

Q. Where in town can visiting Britishers catch up on their cricket?

A. Marine Park in Brooklyn and Flushing Meadows-Corona Park in Queens.

Q. When was the first cricket match held in the city?

A. May 1, 1751. The New Yorkers beat the Londoners.

Q. Long before Disneyland, where did families from all over the country go for exciting rides, shows, and water sports?

A. Coney Island.

Q. How long is the ride on the Cyclone roller coaster in Coney Island?

A. One minute and fifty seconds.

Sports & Leisure

Q. Who invented the Parachute Jump in Coney Island?

A. James H. Strong.

Q. New Yorkers of yesteryear who preferred to swim indoors would visit the luxurious, mirror-lined pool in what Brooklyn hotel?

A. The St. George.

Q. Who made the first parachute jump from a flying vehicle, landing safely in Vauxhall Gardens on Lafayette Street in 1819?

A. Charles Guille.

Q. In 1958, a year the Yankees won the World Series, what New Yorker became a national champion in a game for single players?

A. Chess player Bobby Fischer.

Q. Madison Square Garden is the site of annual contests for members of what other species?

A. The Westminster Kennel Club Dog Show, the International Cat Show, and the National Horse Show.

Q. When was the first Westminster Kennel Club Show?

A. 1877.

Q. At the Westminster Kennel Club Show, what breed has won most championships?

A. Fox terrier.

Q. When was the first New York Marathon, and how many runners participated?

A. In 1970, 126 runners participated.

Q. Who, until his death in 1994, was the director of the New York Marathon?

A. Fred Lebow.

Q. Though ill with cancer, Fred Lebow celebrated his sixtieth birthday by running the New York Marathon in what respectable time?

A. Five hours and thirty-two minutes.

Q. Who, at forty-three, won the women's division of the New York Marathon in 1987?

A. Priscilla Welch.

Q. Runners in the New York Marathon pass through the boroughs in what order?

A. Staten Island, Brooklyn, Queens, Manhattan, the Bronx, and Manhattan again.

Q. It is not as long as the twenty-six miles of the New York Marathon, but what annual race is all uphill?

A. The Empire State Building Run-Up, from the lobby to the eighty-sixth floor.

Q. For athletes who like to see where they have been, what race is held on April Fool's Day in Central Park?

A. The Backwards Mile Race.

Sports & Leisure

Q. The Metropolitan Museum of Art has thousands of old masters from Europe, but it has two hundred thousand of what native product in its collection?

A. Baseball cards.

Q. Since New York City has water on all sides, it is only natural that what local team has won the men's national water polo title the most times?

A. The New York Athletic Club has won twenty-five times.

Q. What, organized in 1844, is the oldest yacht club in the country?

A. New York Yacht Club.

Q. Where can you see the world's largest Raggedy Ann doll?

A. At the Guinness World of Records Exhibition.

Q. The Guinness World of Records Exhibition is located in what record-breaking structure?

A. The Empire State Building.

Q. What enterprise occupies forty-three pages in the Manhattan Yellow Pages?

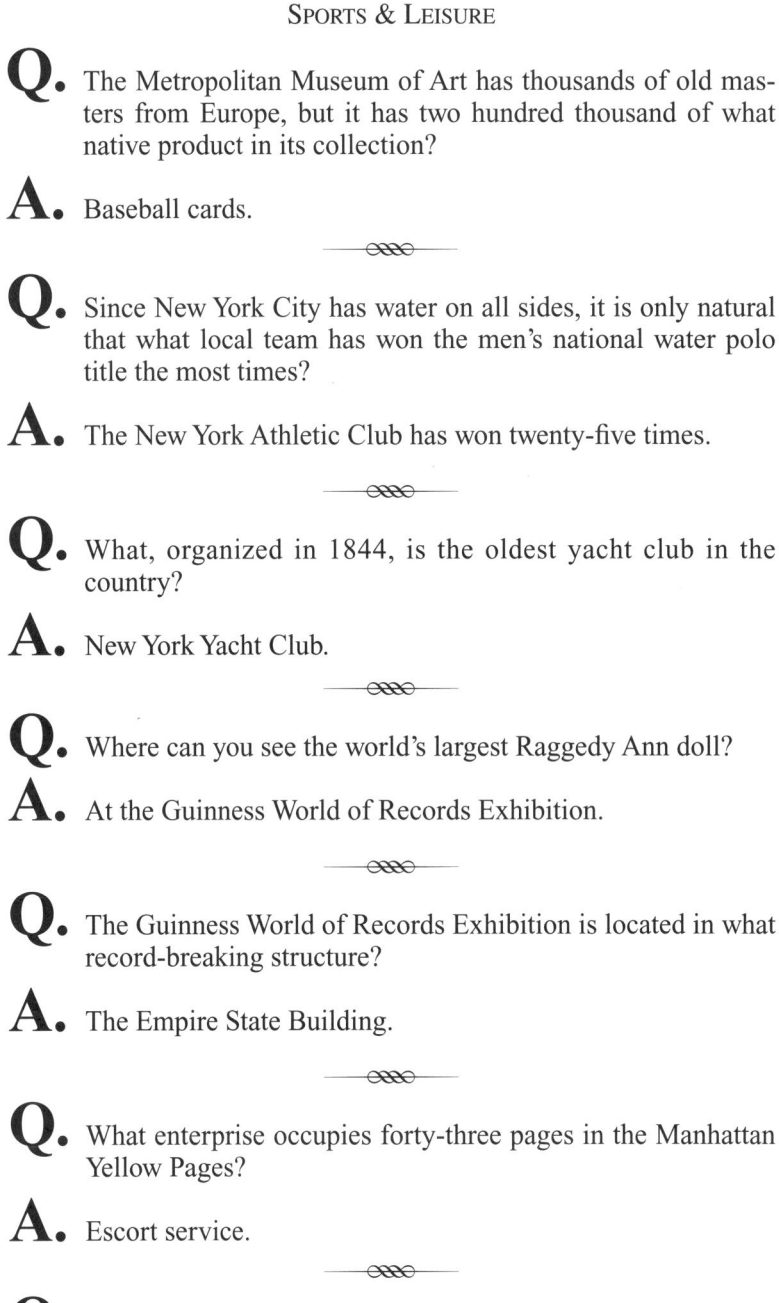

A. Escort service.

Q. At what dance hall did Lower East Sider Arthur Murray win his first dance contest?

A. Grand Central Palace.

Sports & Leisure

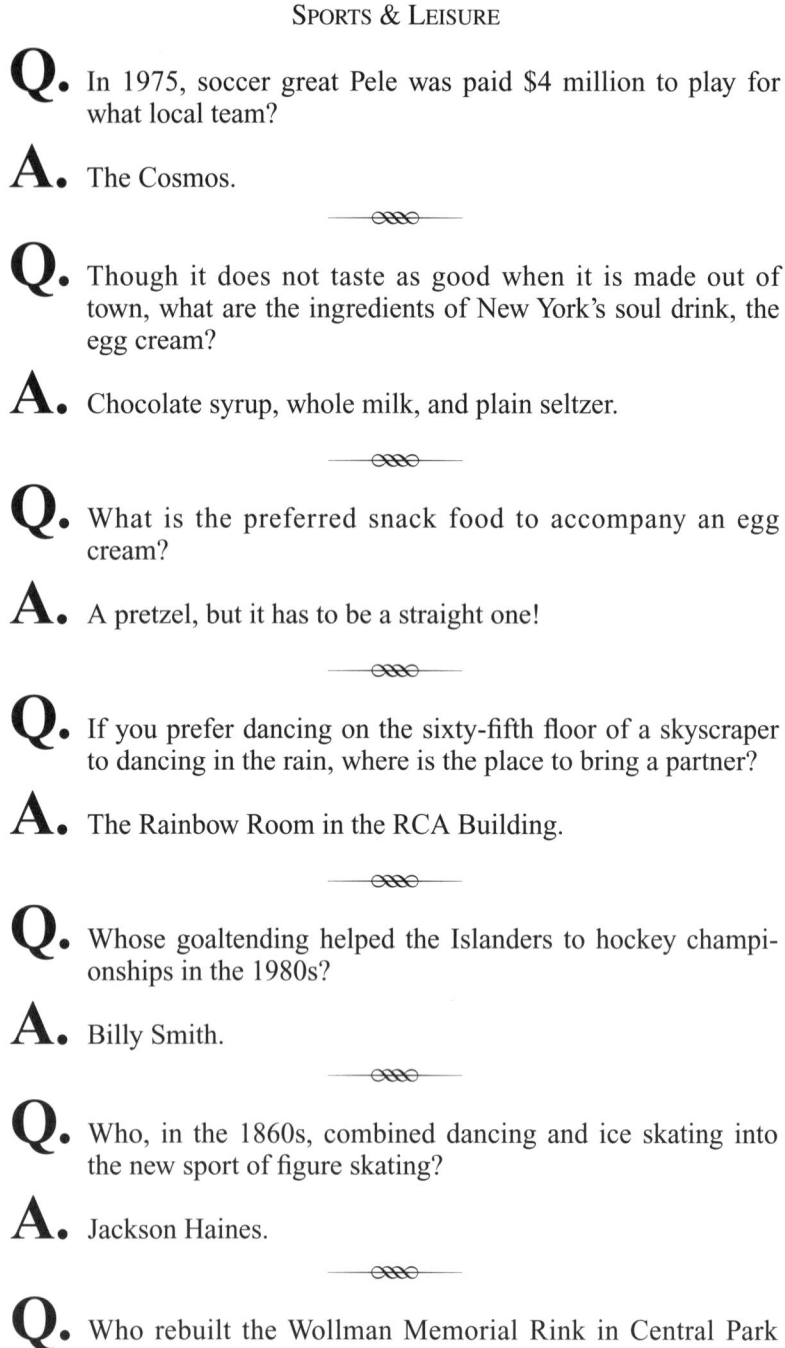

Q. In 1975, soccer great Pele was paid $4 million to play for what local team?

A. The Cosmos.

Q. Though it does not taste as good when it is made out of town, what are the ingredients of New York's soul drink, the egg cream?

A. Chocolate syrup, whole milk, and plain seltzer.

Q. What is the preferred snack food to accompany an egg cream?

A. A pretzel, but it has to be a straight one!

Q. If you prefer dancing on the sixty-fifth floor of a skyscraper to dancing in the rain, where is the place to bring a partner?

A. The Rainbow Room in the RCA Building.

Q. Whose goaltending helped the Islanders to hockey championships in the 1980s?

A. Billy Smith.

Q. Who, in the 1860s, combined dancing and ice skating into the new sport of figure skating?

A. Jackson Haines.

Q. Who rebuilt the Wollman Memorial Rink in Central Park after years of neglect?

A. Donald Trump.

Sports & Leisure

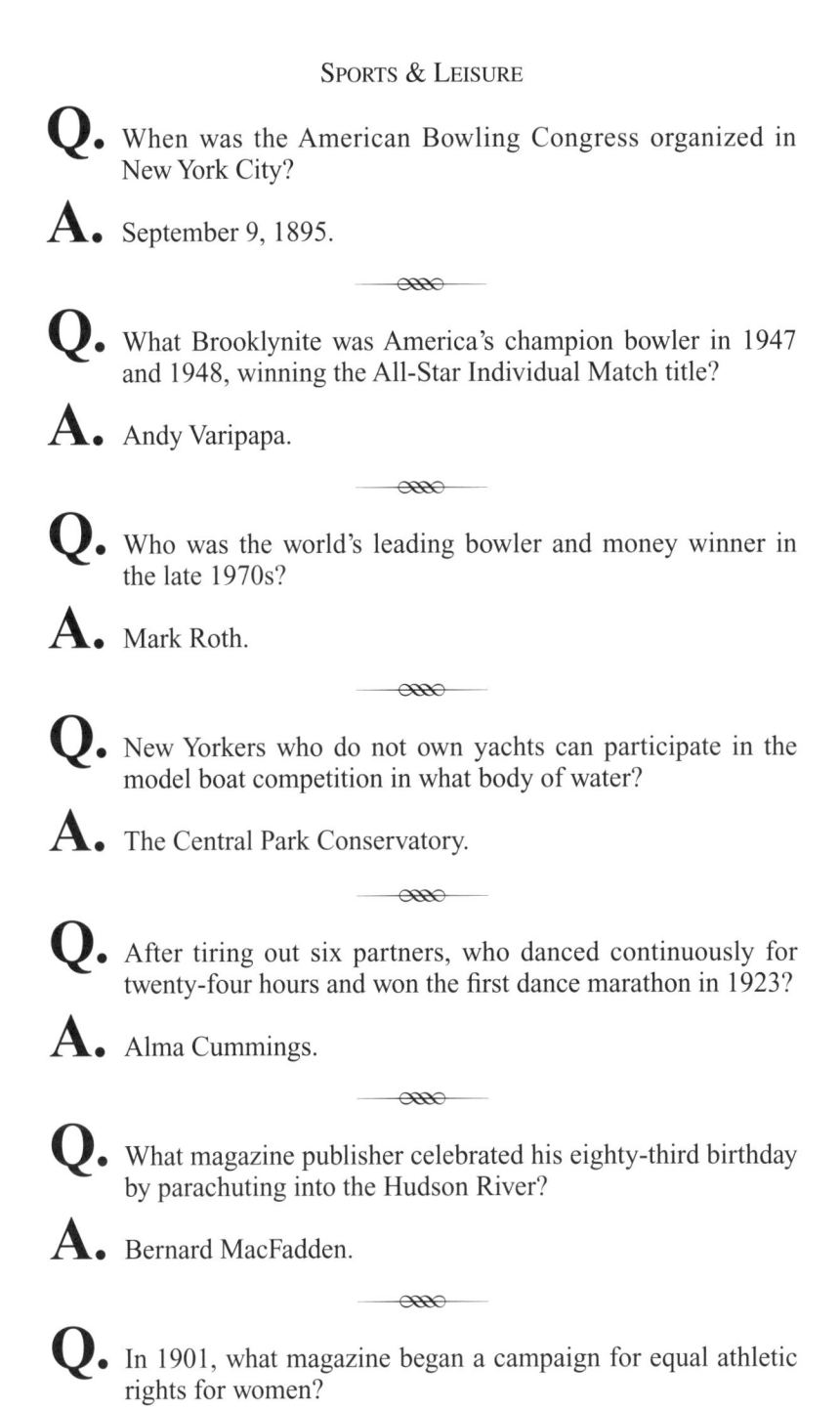

Q. When was the American Bowling Congress organized in New York City?

A. September 9, 1895.

Q. What Brooklynite was America's champion bowler in 1947 and 1948, winning the All-Star Individual Match title?

A. Andy Varipapa.

Q. Who was the world's leading bowler and money winner in the late 1970s?

A. Mark Roth.

Q. New Yorkers who do not own yachts can participate in the model boat competition in what body of water?

A. The Central Park Conservatory.

Q. After tiring out six partners, who danced continuously for twenty-four hours and won the first dance marathon in 1923?

A. Alma Cummings.

Q. What magazine publisher celebrated his eighty-third birthday by parachuting into the Hudson River?

A. Bernard MacFadden.

Q. In 1901, what magazine began a campaign for equal athletic rights for women?

A. *Munsey's.*

Sports & Leisure

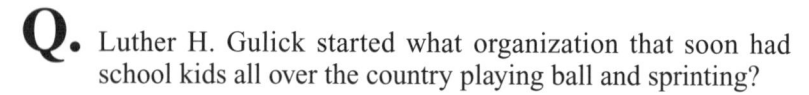

Q. Luther H. Gulick started what organization that soon had school kids all over the country playing ball and sprinting?

A. New York Public School Athletic League in 1903.

Q. What New York organization encourages kids to engage in sports instead of crime?

A. The Police Athletic League.

Q. How many hours after obtaining a New York City marriage license does a couple have to wait before they can use it?

A. Twenty-four hours.

Q. If you are used to traveling with two or more servants, where can you find a special suite to accommodate them?

A. At the Waldorf-Astoria.

Q. At what upscale restaurant, located in a town house, did Richard Nixon and Ronald Reagan discuss their campaign strategies?

A. The Box Tree at 250 East Forty-ninth Street.

Q. To where did Rudolph Valentino, the great silent-screen star, lure visitors when he happened to be in town?

A. The Hotel des Artistes on East Sixty-seventh Street.

Q. At what trendy restaurant do you have to be a celebrity to get a warm welcome?

A. Elaine's at 1703 Second Avenue.

Sports & Leisure

Q. In Paris, the founding father of what Fifth Avenue jewelry store used to design tiaras for Emperor Napoleon to give his wives, though one at a time?

A. Van Cleef & Arpels.

Q. If you're fussy about the right wine for your wild mushroom ravioli, where can you find a restaurant with eight hundred varieties?

A. Windows on the World in the World Trade Center.

Q. Where in town is it possible to buy the same brand of top hat that is worn by British nobility at Buckingham Palace?

A. Bergdorf Goodman Men's, Fifth Avenue at East Fifty-eighth Street.

Q. If diamonds are really a girl's best friend, where is a girl likely to find more friends than anywhere else in the world?

A. The Diamond Center at West Forty-seventh Street between Fifth and Sixth Avenues.

Q. What Lower East Side street is to downscale shoppers what Fifth and Madison Avenues are to upscalers?

A. Orchard Street.

Q. Members of the staff of B. Altman's department store were able to speak with customers in how many languages?

A. Thirty-two.

Q. What free instruction was available at B. Altman's if you bought your materials in the store?

A. In knitting, Wednesday and Thursday from eleven to four.

Sports & Leisure

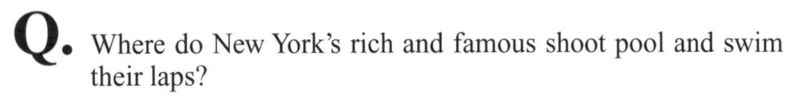

Q. Where do New York's rich and famous shoot pool and swim their laps?

A. The New York Athletic Club and the Downtown Athletic Club.

Q. Legendary billiards wizard Minnesota Fats was portrayed by fellow New Yorker Jackie Gleason in what movie?

A. *The Hustler.*

Q. In 1939, what aviator took off from Floyd Bennett Field and flew by mistake to Dublin instead of California?

A. Douglas "Wrong Way" Corrigan.

Q. What soft drink, named for a borough in New York City, never became as popular as Coke or Pepsi?

A. Manhattan Special.

Q. Until name brands came along, what Brooklyn product was the most popular soft drink for the calorie conscious?

A. Kirsch's No-Cal.

Q. Once reviled as a ninety-seven-pound weakling, what local bodybuilder won the title of World's Most Perfectly Developed Man?

A. Charles Atlas.

Q. Fortified by food from her parents' deli in Manhattan, who was the first woman to swim the thirty-five-mile-wide English Channel, even beating the records of men?

A. Gertrude Ederle, on August 6, 1926. Her time was fourteen hours and thirty-one minutes.

Sports & Leisure

Q. Who was the fastest swimmer around Manhattan Island?

A. Kris Rutford swam it in five hours, fifty-three minutes, and fifty-seven seconds on August 29, 1992.

Q. From where do New Yorkers set out for their serious fishing in the Atlantic Ocean?

A. Sheepshead Bay in Brooklyn.

Q. In 1903, who won the first reported motorcycle race held in the land?

A. George Holden.

Q. What organization of gun fanciers was formed in the city on November 24, 1871?

A. National Rifle Association.

Q. Who, unafraid of heights, suction-cupped his way up the 110 floors of the World Trade Center on May 26, 1977?

A. George Willig.

Q. The world's record for games of hopscotch finished in twenty-four hours is held by what New Yorker?

A. Ashrita Furman, with 307 games.

Q. Versatile Ashrita Furman holds the distance record of 14.99 miles in what sport?

A. Pogo stick jumping.

Sports & Leisure

Q. What new athletic competition for women began in New York in 1980?

A. The World Judo Championship.

Q. In the 1840s, what was a respectable sport for young women?

A. Rolling a hoop.

Q. New York University was the first college to field a team in what sport?

A. Lacrosse, in 1877.

Q. Where can you play miniature golf around models of city landmarks?

A. Gotham Miniature Course in Central Park.

Q. Earlier in the twentieth century, what painter was as famous for his boxing pictures as for his depictions of street life in the city?

A. Reginald Marsh.

Q. Who walked across a tightrope between the two towers of the World Trade Center?

A. Philippe Petit on August 7, 1974.

Q. In what year was the first cup of afternoon tea served at the Palm Court of the Plaza Hotel?

A. 1907.

Sports & Leisure

At the Horn and Hardart Automat, baked beans—with a slice of bacon—was the most popular dish.

Q. At what restaurant chain did even bankers have to stand in line for nickels?

A. The Horn and Hardart Automat.

Q. Costing two whole nickels, what was the most popular dish at the Automat?

A. Baked beans.

Q. When was ready-made ice cream first offered for sale in the city and then the country?

A. June 8, 1786.

Q. In the 1950s and 1960s, after a movie in Times Square, where did a guy take his date for the ultimate in fabulous ice-cream desserts?

A. Toffennetti's Restaurant.

Sports & Leisure

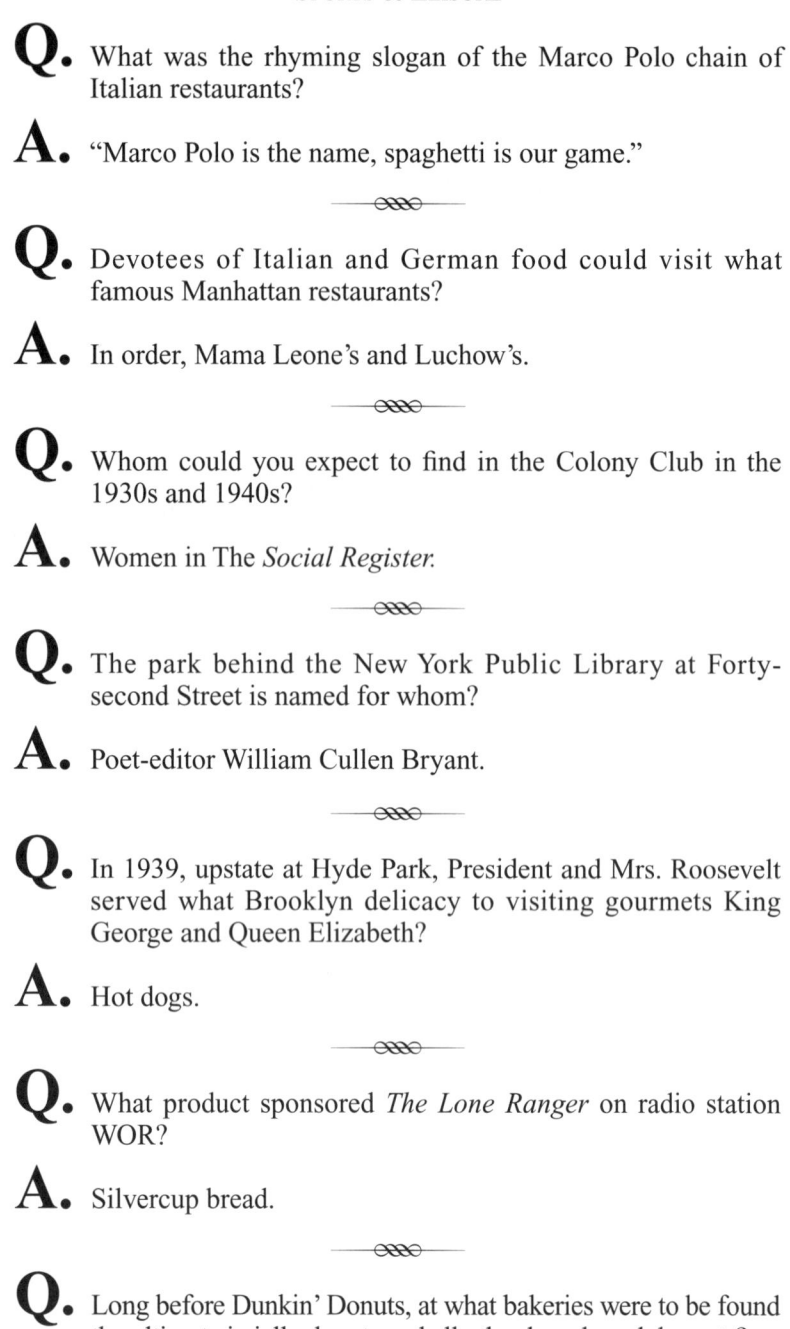

Q. What was the rhyming slogan of the Marco Polo chain of Italian restaurants?

A. "Marco Polo is the name, spaghetti is our game."

Q. Devotees of Italian and German food could visit what famous Manhattan restaurants?

A. In order, Mama Leone's and Luchow's.

Q. Whom could you expect to find in the Colony Club in the 1930s and 1940s?

A. Women in The *Social Register*.

Q. The park behind the New York Public Library at Forty-second Street is named for whom?

A. Poet-editor William Cullen Bryant.

Q. In 1939, upstate at Hyde Park, President and Mrs. Roosevelt served what Brooklyn delicacy to visiting gourmets King George and Queen Elizabeth?

A. Hot dogs.

Q. What product sponsored *The Lone Ranger* on radio station WOR?

A. Silvercup bread.

Q. Long before Dunkin' Donuts, at what bakeries were to be found the ultimate in jelly donuts and all other breads and desserts?

A. Cushman's and Ebinger's.

Sports & Leisure

Q. What bakery delivered bread and muffins to your door at dawn?

A. Dugan's.

Q. Whose ice cream trucks and carts announce the coming of spring in New York?

A. Good Humor and Mister Softee.

Q. Whose Dixie cups of ice cream used to have pictures of glamorous movie stars under the lids?

A. Borden's, Breyer's, Horton's, and Reid's.

Q. If you like a lot of cheese on your hero sandwich, where in New York can you buy two-hundred-pound provolones?

A. Manganaro's at 488 Ninth Avenue.

Q. Before the popularity and availability of air travel, to what nearby mountain resort areas did New Yorkers go for vacation?

A. The Poconos, Adirondacks, and Catskills.

Q. Up in the Catskills, what were the two luxury hotels that offered big-name performers?

A. The Concord and Grossinger's.

Q. Where is the camp for the city's Boy Scouts?

A. Near High Rock Park in Staten Island.

Sports & Leisure

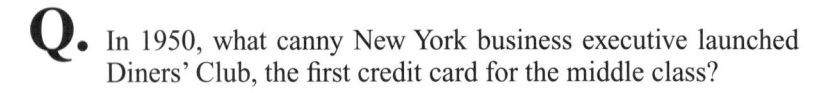

Q. In 1950, what canny New York business executive launched Diners' Club, the first credit card for the middle class?

A. Alfred S. Bloomingdale.

Q. Rodeo fans should check out what Harlem event in May?

A. Black World Championship Rodeo.

Q. What is the cost of a horse-drawn carriage ride through Central Park?

A. Thirty-five dollars for the first half hour and ten dollars for each fifteen minutes after that.

Q. What is a thrifty alternative for romantic New Yorkers who cannot afford a carriage ride through Central Park?

A. The Staten Island ferry, which costs fifty cents for a round trip.

Q. For lovers who like to ride around in circles, there is the Central Park carousel, which was built in what year?

A. 1908.

Q. Where, for the small price of a bus or subway token, can you fly through the air and enjoy a panoramic view of the city?

A. Roosevelt Island Tramway on Second Avenue at East Fifty-ninth Street.

Q. Where, for free, can you see the very first Pooh Bear, Tigger, Piglet, and Eeyore ever stuffed with cuddly material?

A. At Pooh Corner in the Donnell Library at 20 West Fifty-third Street.

SCIENCE & NATURE
CHAPTER SIX

*This is how the flowers grow:
I have watched them and I know.*
—Gabriel Setoun

Q. Laid down at least 120 million years ago, what is the oldest bedrock of the city?

A. Fordham gneiss.

Q. Thanks to what strong rock, laid down later than Fordham gneiss, can tall skyscrapers be erected in the city?

A. Manhattan schist.

Q. Who was the first European botanist to study the flora and fauna of the city?

A. Peter Kalm, in 1748.

Q. What colleague of Peter Kalm, a visiting botanist in 1748, inspired the formation of the Linnaean Society of New York, dedicated to the study of local plants and animal life?

A. Karl von Linné, aka Linnaeus, who began scientific classification.

Science & Nature

Q. Why are so many migratory birds seen in the city?

A. It is under the Atlantic Coastal Flyway.

Q. Where is the Hemlock Grove, all that remains of the city's original forest?

A. At the New York Botanical Garden in the Bronx.

Q. How many species of fish have been seen in local waters?

A. 237.

Q. If you had rather hear bullfrogs than humans, where is the place to go in the fifty-acre Brooklyn Botanic Garden?

A. The lake in the Japanese garden.

Q. What kind of tree inspired Betty Smith to write *A Tree Grows in Brooklyn*?

A. *Ailanthus glandulosa,* or the tree of heaven.

Q. Was Betty Smith, who wrote a popular novel about trees and family life in Brooklyn, born in Brooklyn?

A. Yes, in 1904.

Q. The ginkgo, the city's hardiest street tree, has what other distinction?

A. It is the world's oldest known tree.

Science & Nature

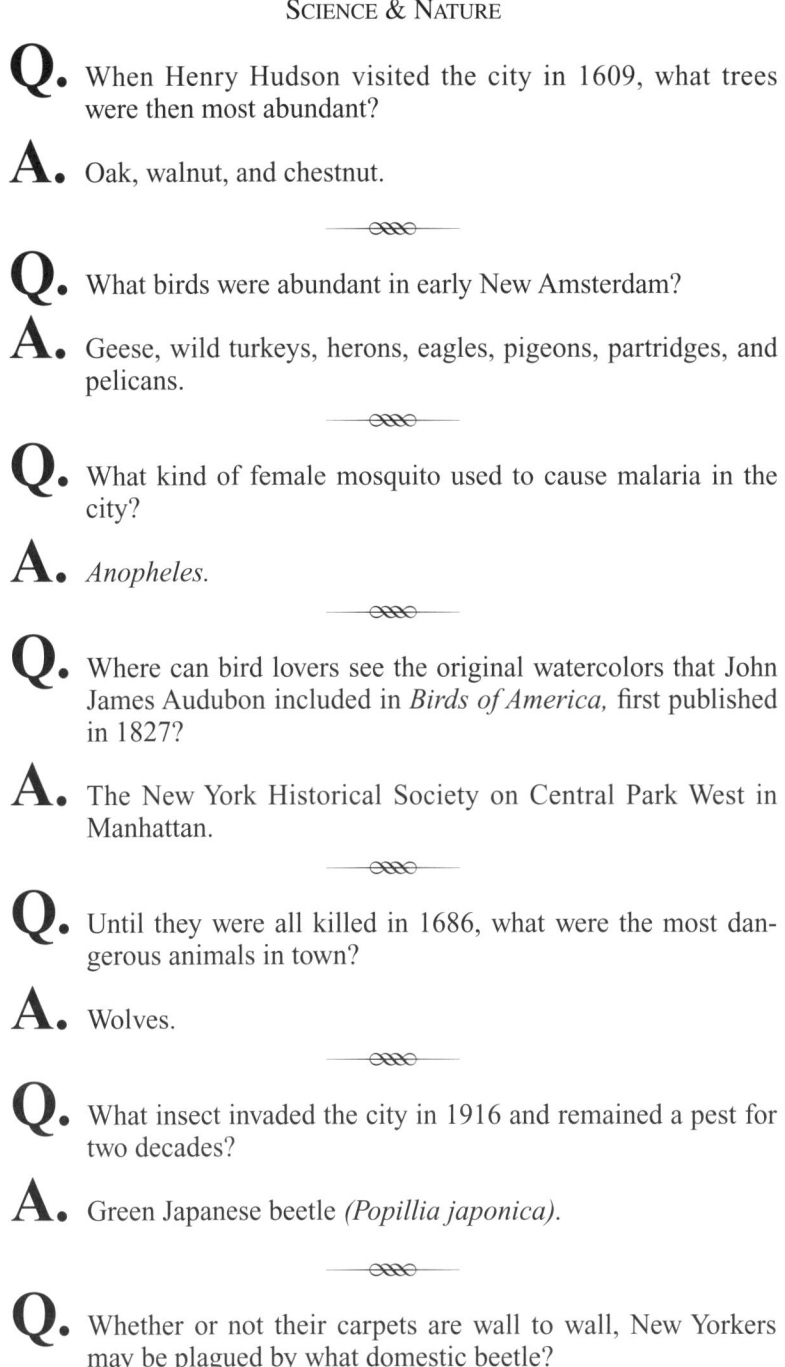

Q. When Henry Hudson visited the city in 1609, what trees were then most abundant?

A. Oak, walnut, and chestnut.

Q. What birds were abundant in early New Amsterdam?

A. Geese, wild turkeys, herons, eagles, pigeons, partridges, and pelicans.

Q. What kind of female mosquito used to cause malaria in the city?

A. *Anopheles.*

Q. Where can bird lovers see the original watercolors that John James Audubon included in *Birds of America,* first published in 1827?

A. The New York Historical Society on Central Park West in Manhattan.

Q. Until they were all killed in 1686, what were the most dangerous animals in town?

A. Wolves.

Q. What insect invaded the city in 1916 and remained a pest for two decades?

A. Green Japanese beetle *(Popillia japonica).*

Q. Whether or not their carpets are wall to wall, New Yorkers may be plagued by what domestic beetle?

A. Black Carpet beetle *(Attagenus piceus).*

Science & Nature

Q. Whether your pet is a mouse or an elephant, to what house of worship can you take it for a blessing the first Sunday in October?

A. The Cathedral of St. John the Divine, Amsterdam Avenue and West 112th Street in Manhattan.

Q. If you are interested in herbs, where can you see a garden with 250 varieties that were popular in the Middle Ages?

A. At the Bonnefont Cloister in Manhattan's Fort Tryon Park.

Q. Who, in 1743, built the country's first successful fire engine?

A. Thomas Lote.

Q. How many species of starfish should you expect to encounter at a city beach?

A. More than a dozen.

Q. From the 1930s through 1957, who offered advice to radio listeners on their marital problems?

A. John J. Anthony, host of *The Good Will Hour.*

Q. Who, in 1767, became the country's first professor of midwifery?

A. John van Brugh of Kings College, now Columbia University.

Q. Abraham Jacobi of Columbia University became the country's first professor of what postnatal specialty in 1870?

A. Pediatrics.

Science & Nature

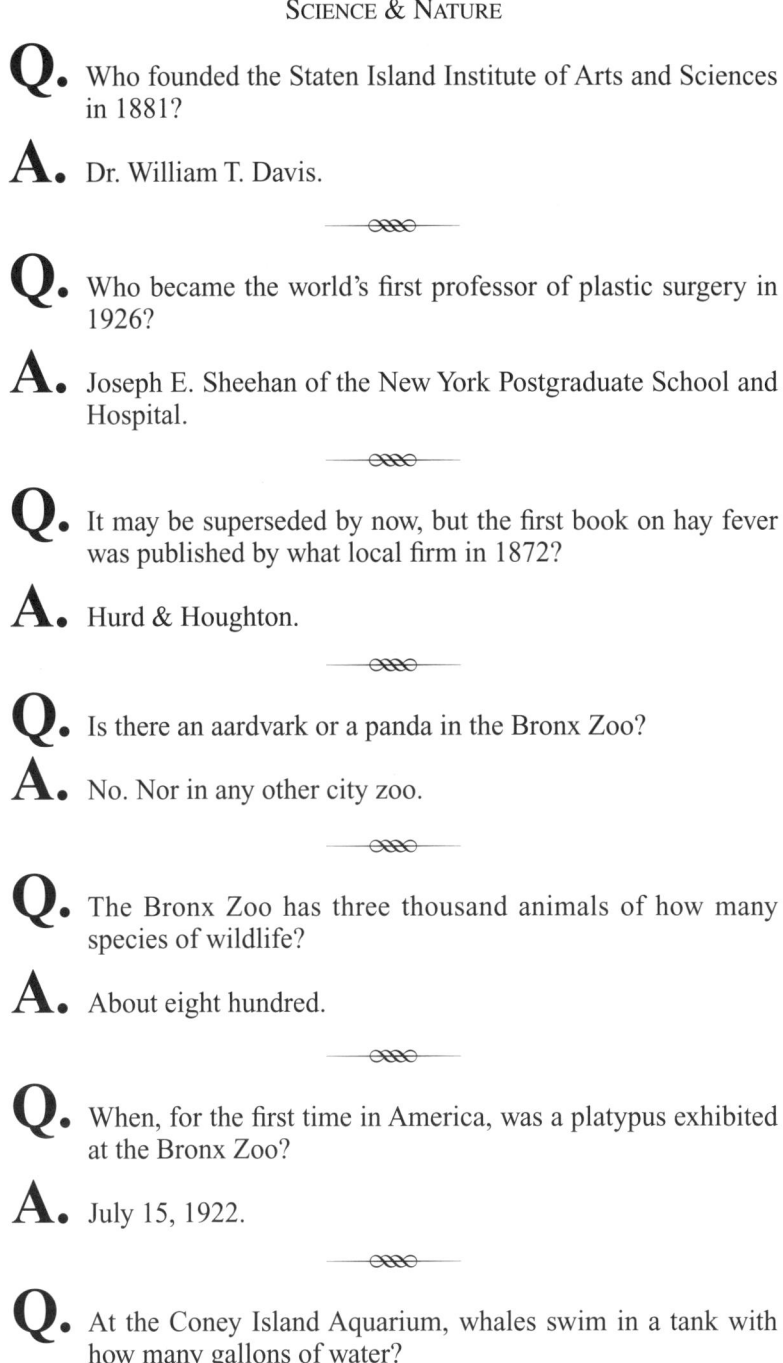

Q. Who founded the Staten Island Institute of Arts and Sciences in 1881?

A. Dr. William T. Davis.

Q. Who became the world's first professor of plastic surgery in 1926?

A. Joseph E. Sheehan of the New York Postgraduate School and Hospital.

Q. It may be superseded by now, but the first book on hay fever was published by what local firm in 1872?

A. Hurd & Houghton.

Q. Is there an aardvark or a panda in the Bronx Zoo?

A. No. Nor in any other city zoo.

Q. The Bronx Zoo has three thousand animals of how many species of wildlife?

A. About eight hundred.

Q. When, for the first time in America, was a platypus exhibited at the Bronx Zoo?

A. July 15, 1922.

Q. At the Coney Island Aquarium, whales swim in a tank with how many gallons of water?

A. 180,000.

Central Park West, one of the most prestigious addresses in New York City. New York Convention and Visitors Bureau.

Q. In what year was Central Park completed and opened to the public?

A. 1876.

Q. Central Park in Manhattan and Prospect Park in Brooklyn are the masterpieces of what two landscape designers?

A. Frederick Law Olmsted and Calvert Vaux.

Q. Until what year did sheep still graze in a Central Park meadow?

A. 1934.

Science & Nature

Q. In addition to its architecture, Belvedere Castle in Central Park offers what daily service to New Yorkers?

A. It is the local station of the National Weather Service.

Q. The Department of Parks and Recreation estimates that how much of the city is parkland?

A. About 25 percent.

Q. About how many trees are there in Central Park?

A. 226,000.

Q. People who tire of feeding pigeons in Central Park have looked up and seen how many other different species of birds?

A. About 270.

Q. How many species of birds have been seen in the Jamaica Bay Wildlife Refuge since it was started in the 1950s?

A. About 330.

Q. What New York park is even bigger than Prospect, Central, and Van Cortlandt Parks combined?

A. Jamaica Bay Wildlife Refuge in Queens has 9,155 acres.

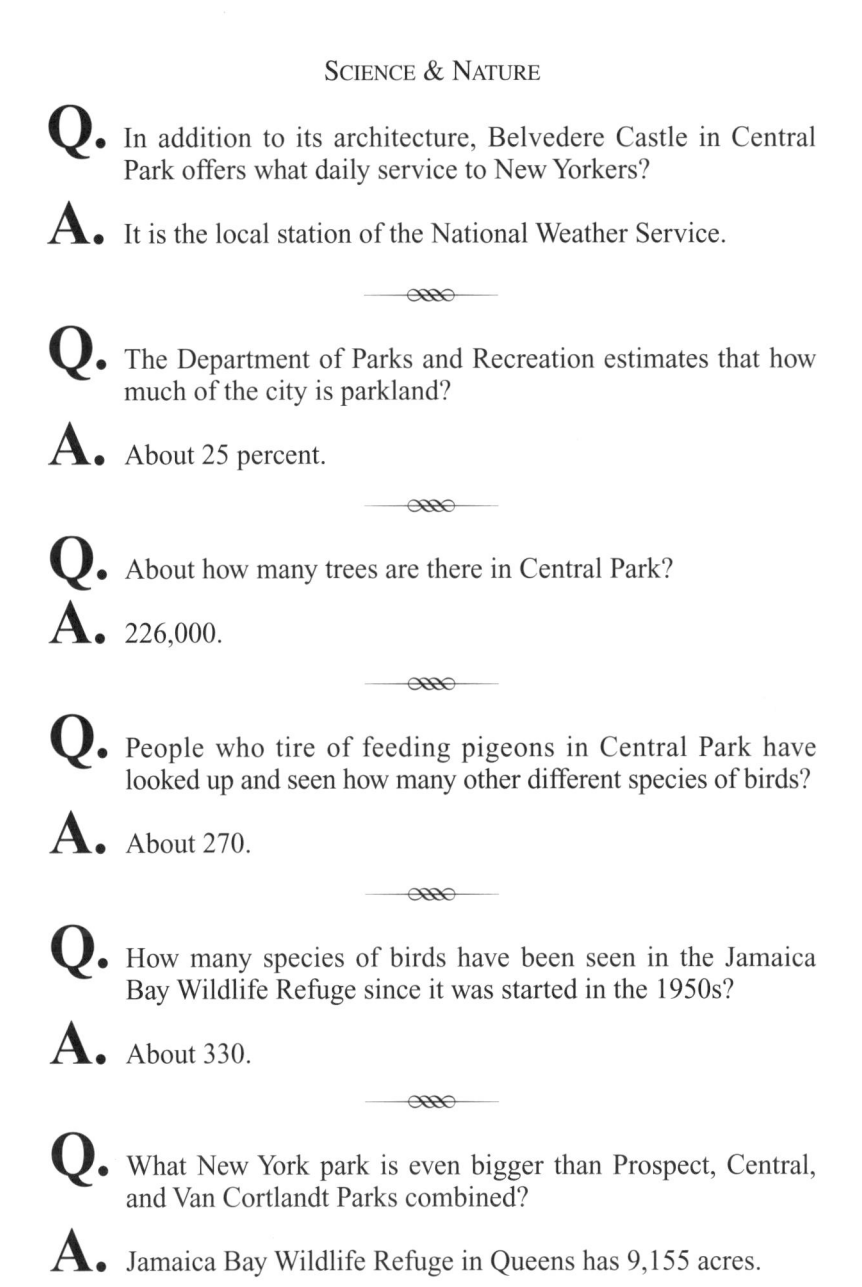

Q. Where in the city can you see a geodesic dome designed by Buckminster Fuller?

A. At the Queens Zoo.

Science & Nature

Q. Where can you see but not touch the oldest and largest collection of bonsai trees in the country?

A. At the Brooklyn Botanic Garden.

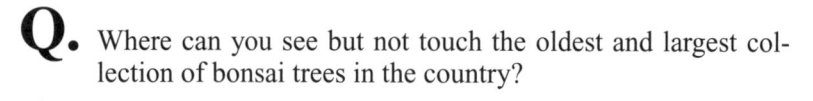

Q. The Brooklyn Botanic Garden has what amenity for people who are visually impaired?

A. A fragrance garden with Braille markers.

Q. How many varieties of roses are there in the Cranford Rose Garden at the Brooklyn Botanic Garden?

A. Nine hundred.

Q. In the Japanese garden at the Brooklyn Botanic Garden, the lotus in the lake is the Buddhist symbol for what?

A. Immortality.

Q. When Henry Waterman invented the elevator in 1850, what did he intend it to transport?

A. Barrels of flour.

Q. President George Washington's dentist, John Greenwood, advanced dentistry in what way?

A. He invented the dental drill in 1790.

Q. What early member of the New York Academy of Science claimed to have a family relationship with primates other than his fellow scientists?

A. Charles Darwin, author of *Origin of Species* and *The Descent of Man*.

Science & Nature

Q. How did New York City became the principal Atlantic port in 1825?

A. With the opening of the Erie Canal, which accessed the Great Lakes and the Midwest.

Q. With 35,825 students, what is the largest private university in the United States?

A. New York University. It was chartered in 1831.

Q. Out-of-towners who miss their raccoons and screech owls are sure to spot quite a few at what wildlife preserve?

A. The Clay Pit Ponds on Staten Island.

Q. Who designed the Brooklyn Bridge, the world's longest suspension bridge at the time it was constructed?

A. John A. Roebling.

Q. What is the official flower of Brooklyn?

A. Forsythia.

Q. If you spot a snake in New York, it is likely to be what harmless species?

A. The brown snake *(Storeria dekayi)*.

Q. Why can nineteenth-century pharmaceutical tycoon Eugene Schieffelin be called the "Bird Man of New York"?

A. He tried to introduce to North America all the birds mentioned in Shakespeare's works.

Science & Nature

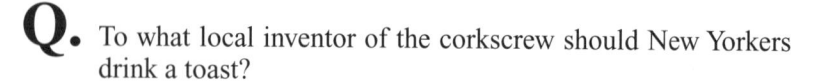

Q. To what local inventor of the corkscrew should New Yorkers drink a toast?

A. M. L. Bryn, in 1860.

Q. Who coined the word "Vaseline" for his refinement of petroleum jelly and then began to sell it in 1870?

A. Robert A. Chesebrough.

Q. In the 1940s, former circus strongman the Mighty Atom sold homemade herbal remedies that he claimed cured what afflictions?

A. Baldness and impotence.

Q. In 1840, what popular local product claimed to heal most human afflictions?

A. Bristol's Fluid Extract of Sarsaparilla.

Q. Before calling their doctors, many New Yorkers first consult a book on health and nutrition by what columnist of the *New York Times*?

A. Jane Brody.

Q. Who, with radio talks from 1957 to 1987, was a pioneer in teaching about vitamins and minerals, rest and exercise, nutritious food and junk food?

A. Carlton Fredericks.

Q. If you have learned the difference between good and bad cholesterol and how to keep them in balance, it is thanks to whose research?

A. 1985 Nobel Prize winner Michael S. Brown.

Science & Nature

Q. Gertrude Elion, 1988 Nobel Prize winner in medicine, was a graduate of what free municipal college?

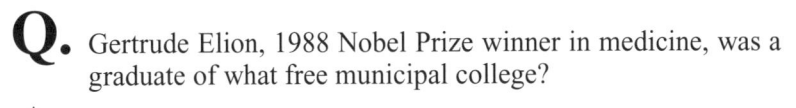

A. Hunter College.

Q. What was the country's first college to ban discrimination because of race, color, or religion?

A. Cooper Union, in 1851.

Q. In 1992, a pair of peregrine falcons took up residence in what Park Avenue skyscraper?

A. The Metropolitan Life Building.

Q. Dr. Lewis Thomas, winner of the National Book Award for *The Lives of a Cell,* was president of what hospital?

A. Memorial Sloan-Kettering Cancer Center.

Q. What public health expert established and headed the Women's Medical Society of New York?

A. Dr. Anna Williams.

Q. The country's first school of nursing was established at what municipal hospital in 1873?

A. Bellevue.

Q. Stuyvesant High School and the Bronx High School of Science have long dominated the finals of what national competition?

A. The Westinghouse Science Talent Search.

SCIENCE & NATURE

Q. Where is the city's wildlife sanctuary?

A. Jamaica Bay in Gateway National Park.

Q. In addition to Jamaica Bay in Brooklyn, what and where are the other parts of Gateway National Park, established in 1972?

A. Raritan Bay on Staten Island and Breezy Point in Rockaway, Queens.

Q. In February 1959 at Jamaica Bay, what European bird was spotted for the first time in North America?

A. The redwing thrush.

Q. At the Queens Museum, what does the *Panorama,* the world's largest scale model, depict?

A. The five boroughs and their important buildings and natural features.

Q. Who patented the stenotype machine in 1876?

A. John C. Zachos.

Q. Who invented the electrical hearing aid in 1901?

A. Miller R. Hutchinson.

Q. Created in 1979, what group conducts free nature tours of the city's parks?

A. The Urban Park Rangers.

Science & Nature

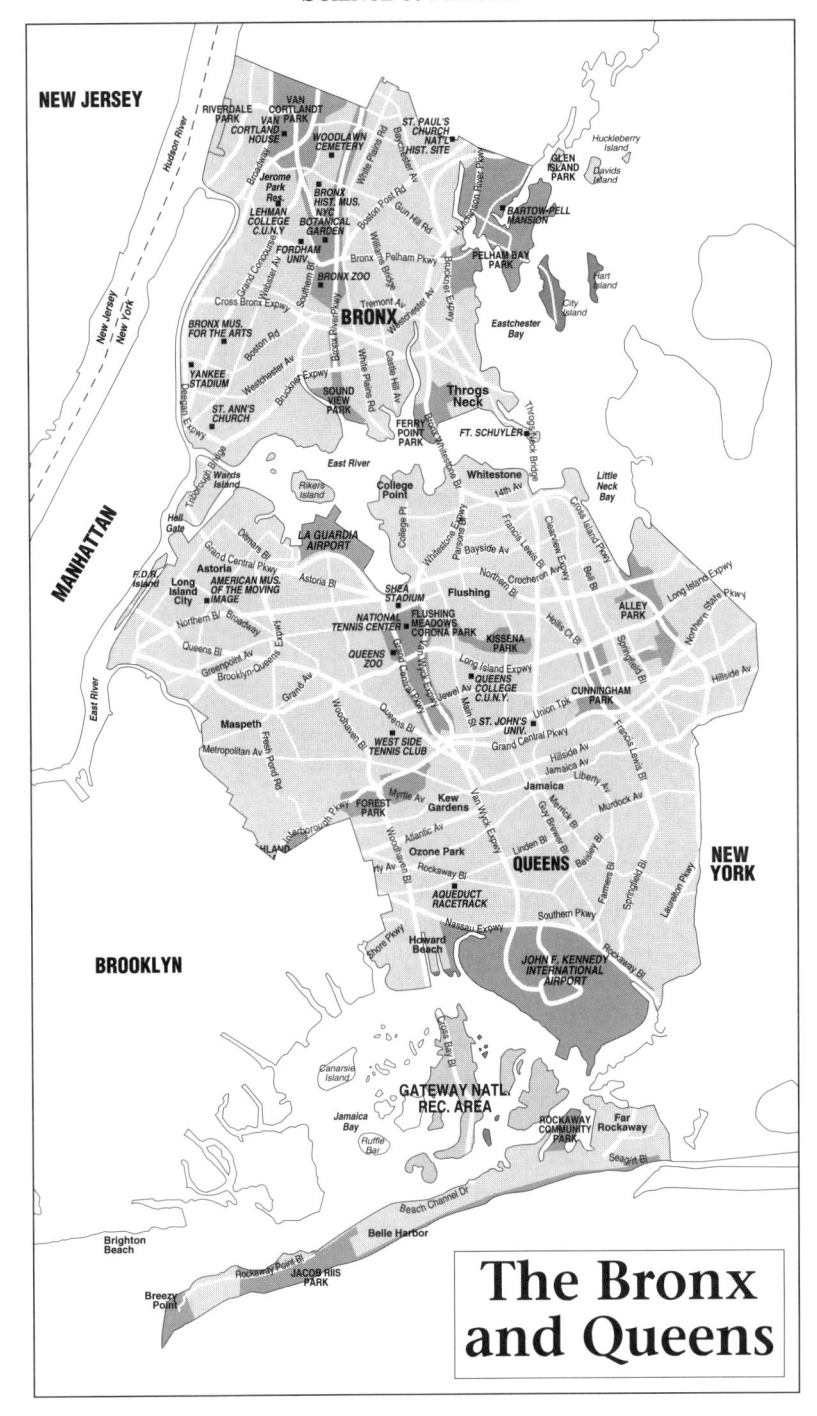

The Bronx and Queens

Science & Nature

Q. What was the contribution to medicine of Dr. Gladys Hobby?

A. She prepared and tested the first penicillin in the United States.

Q. Who was the first head of the Division of Child Hygiene, later the Bureau of Child Health?

A. Dr. Josephine Baker.

Q. How do some New Yorkers try to keep the city's seven hundred thousand pigeons off their roofs?

A. With plastic owls.

Q. Where in Brooklyn can visiting sportsmen observe but not hunt pheasants?

A. Marine Park.

Q. What was the name of the woodchuck that took up residence in Central Park in the 1980s?

A. Phyllis.

Q. In 1866, at the Women's Hospital of the State of New York, Dr. James Sims performed what procedure for the first time?

A. Artificial insemination.

Q. Who was the country's first teacher of lip-reading to people who were deaf?

A. Sarah W. Keeler in 1882.

Science & Nature

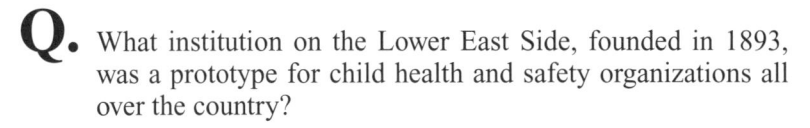

Q. What institution on the Lower East Side, founded in 1893, was a prototype for child health and safety organizations all over the country?

A. The Henry Street Settlement, established by Lillian Wald.

Q. Who was inventing the telegraph when he was not teaching art at New York University?

A. Samuel F. B. Morse.

Q. Who, in 1916, established America's first birth control clinic in Brooklyn?

A. Margaret Sanger.

Q. The country's first eye bank was established at what hospital in 1944?

A. New York Hospital.

Q. In what Bronx hospital did Dr. Oliver Sacks treat the patients described in the book and film *Awakenings*?

A. Montefiore.

Q. What high school in the country has the most (six) Nobel Prize winners?

A. The Bronx High School of Science.

Q. Who invented the valve that operates such aerosol products as whipped cream and insect repellent?

A. Robert H. Abplanalp, in 1952.

Science & Nature

Q. At the World's Fair of 1939, what all-important invention was introduced to the public?

A. Television.

Q. What researcher developed a vaccine for polio in 1952?

A. Dr. Jonas Salk.

Q. What New Yorker built the world's first seagoing steamboat in 1806?

A. John Stevens.

Q. What New Yorker always has an answer for the emotional problems of radio listeners and magazine readers?

A. Dr. Joyce Brothers.

Q. If your emotional problem is mostly sexual, whose books and radio programs will offer you corrective insights?

A. Dr. Ruth Westheimer.

Q. What boy from Brooklyn became equally at home in the cosmos?

A. Astronomer-author-television star Carl Sagan.

Q. Whose statue stands on the steps of the American Museum of Natural History?

A. Theodore Roosevelt.

Science & Nature

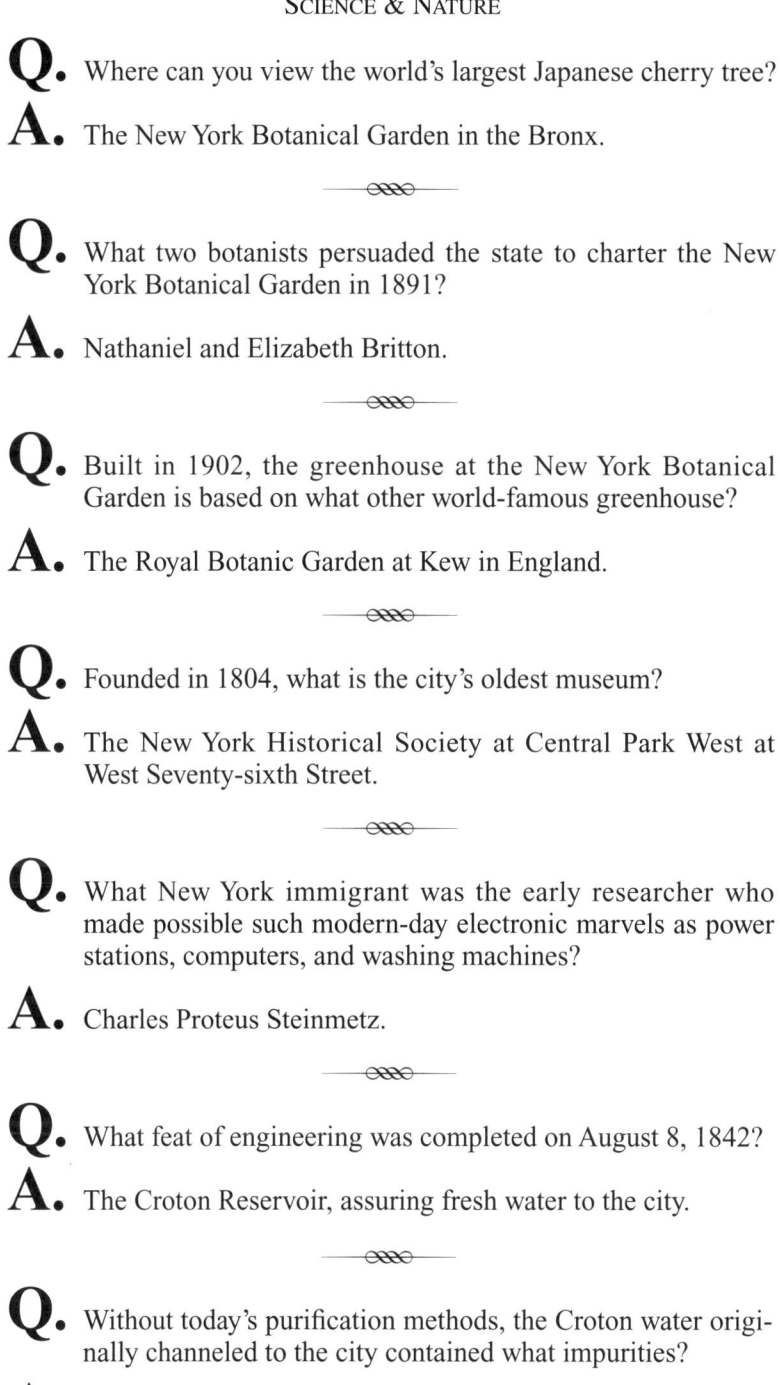

Q. Where can you view the world's largest Japanese cherry tree?

A. The New York Botanical Garden in the Bronx.

Q. What two botanists persuaded the state to charter the New York Botanical Garden in 1891?

A. Nathaniel and Elizabeth Britton.

Q. Built in 1902, the greenhouse at the New York Botanical Garden is based on what other world-famous greenhouse?

A. The Royal Botanic Garden at Kew in England.

Q. Founded in 1804, what is the city's oldest museum?

A. The New York Historical Society at Central Park West at West Seventy-sixth Street.

Q. What New York immigrant was the early researcher who made possible such modern-day electronic marvels as power stations, computers, and washing machines?

A. Charles Proteus Steinmetz.

Q. What feat of engineering was completed on August 8, 1842?

A. The Croton Reservoir, assuring fresh water to the city.

Q. Without today's purification methods, the Croton water originally channeled to the city contained what impurities?

A. Tadpoles and other animalcula.

Science & Nature

🍎 EAU DE NEW YORK

When you go to New York City, you *can* drink the water. In fact, New Yorkers drink up to 1.5 billion gallons of water daily—that's enough to fill 2,100 Olympic swimming pools. One reason New Yorkers drink so much is because the city boasts some of the best-tasting water in the world. Some say it's even better than bottled water, and city chefs claim it has a "fruity" bouquet.

Where does all this water come from? New York City's water is carried from the Croton River, the Catskills, and the Delaware River through a network of more than six thousand miles of aqueducts, tunnels, and water mains. The water is gathered into eighteen reservoirs holding as much as 550 billion gallons.

The only way for that water to reach the city is through two tunnels. The first opened in 1917, the second in 1937, and despite their age, the concrete tunnels have never been inspected. Today they carry 60 percent more water than they were designed to bear originally. Engineers say there could be leaks, and chunks of concrete may have fallen into the tunnels, but they cannot shut down either tunnel for inspection or repairs because the other tunnel could not by itself bear the burden of the city's entire water supply. Since the valves have never been closed, experts do not know if it is even possible to turn them off, or if they could open the system again once they shut it down. The city might lose its water supply for up to eighteen months.

Showing foresight, the city did begin to work on a third tunnel in 1970 to allow one of the older tunnels to be shut down, inspected, and repaired. A massive endeavor, the project uses a device called a hole borer that acts like a huge can opener to dig a twenty-foot-diameter hole in the solid rock beneath the city. Already, parts of tunnel #3 are in service. A valve chamber the size of two football fields sits ten stories under Van Cortlandt Park in the Bronx. The city finished the first section in 1993, and the entire project is scheduled for completion in 2020. Until then, New York still depends on the two original tunnels for its water supply. Drink up and enjoy some eau de New York!

Science & Nature

Q. Where in New York can you see a Mouse House?
A. The Bronx Zoo.

Q. Under whose leadership did RCA develop the compact disc?
A. Robert W. Sarnoff.

Q. If a cat needs psychotherapy, who is the expert to visit in New York?
A. Carole Wilbourn, author of *Cat on the Couch.*

Q. In 1940, what world-famous mathematician-philosopher was considered morally unfit to teach in the City College of New York?
A. Bertrand Russell.

Q. Bertrand Russell was defended on the charge of moral turpitude by what philosopher-educator from Columbia University?
A. John Dewey.

Q. Professor Harold C. Urey of Columbia University received the Nobel Prize in 1934 for what discovery?
A. Heavy water.

Q. With the publication of *The Mind of Primitive Man* in 1911, who became the most famous anthropologist in the country?
A. Franz Boas.

SCIENCE & NATURE

Q. What southern college, famed for discoveries in science and medicine, was established by a Yankee from Staten Island?

A. Vanderbilt University in Nashville, opened in 1875 after a $1 million dollar gift from Cornelius Vanderbilt.

Q. At a pier on Cortlandt Street in 1807, who demonstrated a steamboat called the *Clermont*?

A. Robert Fulton.

Q. Electric bulbs for Christmas trees were invented in 1882 by what associate of Thomas Edison?

A. Edward H. Johnson.

Q. Who invented the coal stove?

A. Jordan Mott.

Q. In 1896, where was the first escalator installed?

A. Old Iron Pier in Coney Island.

Q. In 1889, who designed the first computer for data processing?

A. Dr. Herman Hollerith.

Q. Already America's top seismologist, what Brooklynite became chief scientific advisor to President Carter?

A. Frank Press.

Science & Nature

Q. Maybe he was hiding from someone, but what New York chemist developed the science of camouflage for the U.S. armed forces?

A. Maximillian Toch.

Q. The jet fuels that propel spaceships were developed by what scientist from an African-American ghetto section of the Bronx?

A. Dr. Albert C. Antoine.

Q. What great naturalist saw his last birds from the lawn of his Upper Manhattan residence near the Hudson River?

A. John James Audubon (1785–1851).

Q. In 1841, what New Yorker invented a cork life preserver that was the best of its time?

A. Napoleon E. Guerin.

Q. First demonstrated by NBC in 1947, the zoom lens was invented by what New Yorker?

A. Dr. Frank G. Back.

Q. If you ever got a low IQ score because you flunked the block matching, you should blame what psychologist?

A. Samuel C. Kohs.

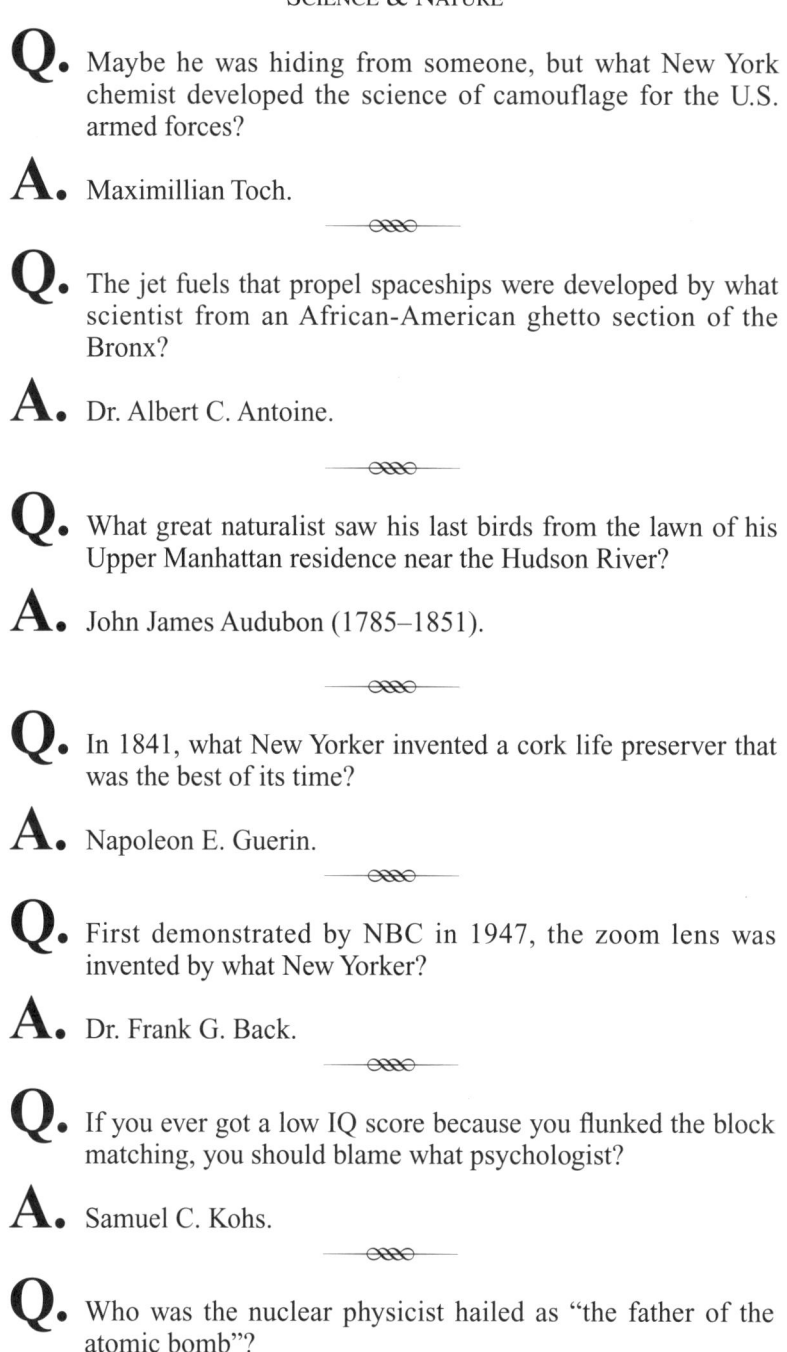

Q. Who was the nuclear physicist hailed as "the father of the atomic bomb"?

A. J. Robert Oppenheimer.

Science & Nature

Q. Where was the world's first atomic pile built?
A. Columbia University.

Q. *Coming of Age in Samoa,* a surprise bestseller in 1928, was written by what ethnologist at the American Museum of Natural History?
A. Margaret Mead.

Q. In 1946, Dr. Benjamin Spock published what all-time best-selling health book?
A. *The Common Sense Book of Baby and Child Care.*

Q. For what book did René Dubos, professor of pathology and microbiology at Rockefeller University, win a Pulitzer Prize in 1969?
A. *So Human an Animal.*

Q. Without what New Yorker would there be no frozen foods?
A. Clarence Birdseye.

Q. Who invented FM radio?
A. Edwin H. Armstrong.

Q. In 1977, what Bronxite won the Nobel Prize for developing radioactive isotopes to treat cancer?
A. Rosalyn Yalow.

Science & Nature

Q. Who established the nation's first large-scale horticultural nursery?

A. William Prince of Flushing in Queens in 1737.

Q. Who invented chewing gum in 1872?

A. Thomas Adams of Staten Island.

Q. During the Civil War, who designed the *Monitor*, the ironclad warship for the Union navy?

A. John Ericsson.

Q. Long before the Internet, Maspeth in Queens was a center of what all-natural form of communication?

A. Training of homing pigeons.

Q. What Bronx school, founded in 1831, was one of the first in the country to educate children who were both blind and deaf?

A. New York Institute for the Education of the Blind.

Q. Who invented the rotary printing press?

A. Richard M. Hoe in 1846.

Q. How and where in New York City did H. J. Heinz get the inspiration for his trademark of fifty-seven varieties of food products?

A. Riding an elevated train, he spotted an ad for twenty-one styles of shoes.

Science & Nature

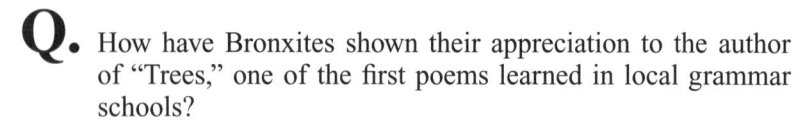

Q. How have Bronxites shown their appreciation to the author of "Trees," one of the first poems learned in local grammar schools?

A. With the establishment of Joyce Kilmer Park on the Grand Concourse.

Q. Shakespeare never visited the Big Apple, but where can you see gardens with the flowers mentioned in his plays?

A. Central Park and the Brooklyn Botanic Garden.

Q. In the 1930s and 1940s, what master builder transformed the city with new bridges, highways, parks, and beaches?

A. Parks Commissioner Robert Moses.

Q. When he was not rooting for the Dodgers, what Brooklynite found time to synthesize DNA in 1956 and then win a Nobel Prize in 1959?

A. Arthur Kornberg.

Q. For what research did Richard Feynman of Queens win the Nobel Prize in 1965?

A. Quantum electrodynamics.

Q. Who coined the word *quark* and won the 1969 Nobel Prize for his work on subatomic particles?

A. Murray Gell-Mann.

Q. How did James A. Church help rid the country of both dirt and indigestion in 1867?

A. By starting the Arm & Hammer Baking Soda Company.

Science & Nature

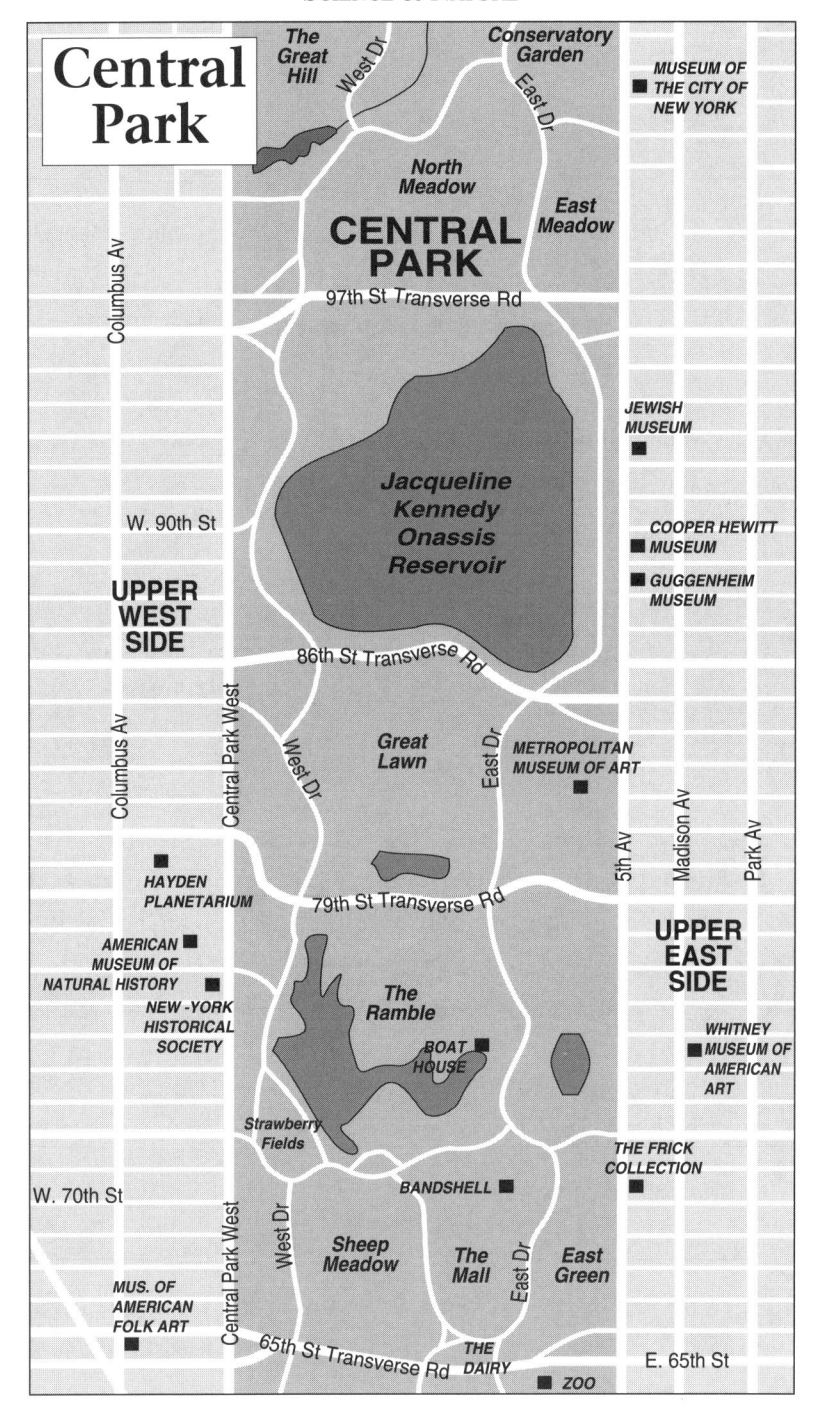

Central Park

- The Great Hill
- Conservatory Garden
- MUSEUM OF THE CITY OF NEW YORK
- West Dr
- East Dr
- North Meadow
- East Meadow

CENTRAL PARK

97th St Transverse Rd

- Columbus Av
- W. 90th St
- **UPPER WEST SIDE**
- Jacqueline Kennedy Onassis Reservoir
- JEWISH MUSEUM
- COOPER HEWITT MUSEUM
- GUGGENHEIM MUSEUM

86th St Transverse Rd

- Central Park West
- West Dr
- Great Lawn
- East Dr
- METROPOLITAN MUSEUM OF ART
- Columbus Av
- 5th Av
- Madison Av
- Park Av
- HAYDEN PLANETARIUM

79th St Transverse Rd

- AMERICAN MUSEUM OF NATURAL HISTORY
- NEW-YORK HISTORICAL SOCIETY
- **UPPER EAST SIDE**
- The Ramble
- BOAT HOUSE
- WHITNEY MUSEUM OF AMERICAN ART
- Strawberry Fields
- THE FRICK COLLECTION
- W. 70th St
- BANDSHELL
- Central Park West
- West Dr
- Sheep Meadow
- The Mall
- East Dr
- East Green
- MUS. OF AMERICAN FOLK ART

65th St Transverse Rd

- THE DAIRY
- ZOO
- E. 65th St

Science & Nature

Q. William Sheppard invented what household product in 1865?

A. Liquid soap.

Q. Elizabeth and Emily Blackwell founded what pioneer institution in 1868?

A. The New York Infirmary for Women and Children.

Q. What local firm made the first flashlights in 1898?

A. American Electric and Novelty Manufacturing Company. It later changed its name to Eveready.

Q. Who designed the Hoover vacuum cleaner, the Honeywell wall thermometer, and the first anatomically correct toilet seat?

A. Henry Dreyfuss.

Q. What geneticist from Brooklyn served with the Atomic Energy Commission and became president of Radcliffe College?

A. Dr. Mary Bunting.

Q. Who invented powdered milk?

A. Samuel R. Percy in 1872.

Q. What company was the first in the country to pasteurize milk?

A. Sheffield Farms of New York City in 1895.

Science & Nature

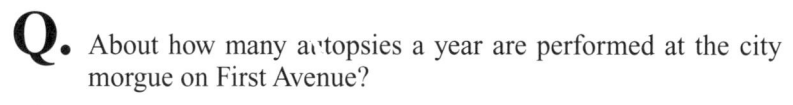

Q. About how many autopsies a year are performed at the city morgue on First Avenue?

A. 8,500.

Q. Long before Pampers, whose safety pins kept the nation's diapers in place?

A. Walter Hunt since 1849.

Q. What, founded in 1899, was the world's first science museum for the young?

A. The Brooklyn Children's Museum, now at 145 Brooklyn Avenue.

Q. What device did Isaac Singer patent in 1851?

A. A sewing machine with a rocking treadle.

Q. What commercial building in Lower Manhattan installed the world's first hydraulic elevator in 1870?

A. The Equitable Building.

Q. What is the only school in the country that offers a master's degree in forensic psychology?

A. John Jay College of Criminal Justice in Manhattan.

Q. Who won the 1946 Nobel Prize for work in mutations and genetics?

A. Herman J. Muller.

Science & Nature

Q. Who was the first woman doctor at the White House?

A. Dr. Janet G. Travell, personal physician to President Kennedy.

Q. What was the first newspaper in the country to microfilm past issues?

A. The *New York Times*.

Q. In 1968, who won the Nobel Prize for unscrambling the genetic code?

A. Marshall Nirenberg.

Q. What immunologist won the 1972 Nobel Prize for research on antibodies and gamma globulin?

A. Gerald M. Edelman.

Q. Maybe dissatisfied with human intelligence in his hometown, who became a world-class expert in artificial intelligence?

A. Professor Marvin Minsky.

Q. If you spot a shark in local waters, it is likely to be what species?

A. Brown shark *(Cacharias milberti)*.

Q. What Brooklynite, living close to cold blasts from the ocean, invented the auto heater?

A. Augusta M. Rogers.

Science & Nature

Q. Who invented the air conditioner?
A. Willis Carrier.

Q. If spaceships give you claustrophobia, what is a more comfortable way to visit Mars and the Moon?
A. The Hayden Planetarium at Central Park West and West Eighty-first Street.

Q. What faculty member of New York University in the 1830s invented "the gun that won the West" for the United States?
A. Samuel Colt.

Q. Who, in 1839, took the first photograph of the moon?
A. Professor John William Draper.

Q. Where is the city's first and only funeral parlor for pets?
A. All Pets Go to Heaven, Inc., on Carroll Street in Brooklyn. Established in 1997 by Raymond Leone.

Q. What mathematician was the first woman president of the American Association for the Advancement of Science?
A. Mina Spiegel Rees.

Q. When was Earth Day first observed in the city?
A. April 22, 1970.

Science & Nature

Q. Sports columnist and radio personality John Kieran wrote what indispensable book about the flora and fauna of the city?

A. *A Natural History of New York City.*

Q. Where is the John Kieran Nature Trail?

A. Van Cortlandt Park in the Bronx.

Q. What and when was the first international exposition held in the country?

A. The New York World's Fair of 1853.

Q. In 1869, which of the fifty-seven Heinz varieties could New Yorkers first purchase?

A. Horseradish.

Q. What graduate of Erasmus High in Brooklyn invented the gyroscope and the gyrocompass, essential for the stability of ships, planes, and submarines?

A. Elmer Sperry.

Q. Established in the Riverdale section of the Bronx is what institution devoted to nature studies?

A. The Wave Hill Center for Environmental Studies.

Q. Where can butterflies find a garden with plants especially nourishing for them?

A. Snug Harbor in Staten Island.

Science & Nature

Q. What Brooklyn pharmacist invented the Band-Aid?
A. Robert Johnson.

Q. Who, unwarned by a surgeon general, invented the first machine to make cigarettes?
A. Albert H. Hook, in 1872.

Q. The country's first department of library science was established by Melvil Dewey at what local school in 1889?
A. Columbia University.

Q. Who established the country's first blood bank in New York?
A. Robert C. Drew in 1940.

Q. When did C. O. Bigelow's, the nation's oldest apothecary, open on Sixth Avenue in Greenwich Village?
A. 1838.

Q. Where can you see specimens of all the minerals ever dug up in the city?
A. The Hall of Gems at the American Museum of Natural History.

Q. Why is Soho in Manhattan called Silicon Valley East?
A. Because of its concentration of software programmers.

Science & Nature

Q. How many dogs are there in New York, where licensing has been mandatory since 1894?

A. About one million, according to the ASPCA.

Q. For all the good it has done, when was a cleanup law for dogs passed in the city?

A. 1978.

Q. When Pandora came to town on June 10, 1938, where did she take up residence without having to pay rent?

A. Pandora, a giant panda, became a star attraction at the Bronx Zoo.

Q. Where can you see free spectacular flower shows in April?

A. Indoors, at R. H. Macy's. Outdoors, at Rockefeller Plaza and the World Financial Center.

Q. What great benefactor of children young and old invented the toy electric train in 1900?

A. Joshua Lionel Cowen, who later headed the company that made Lionel trains.